# El Charro Café

# El Charro Café

## The Tastes and Traditions of Tucson

Carlotta Dunn Flores

FISHER
BOOKS

Dedicated to my mother, Zarina Flores Dunn; my husband, Ray; my children, Raymon, Marques and Candace; my sisters, Wilma and Sandy; my extended families, friends and customers who have made El Charro part of their tradition, as well as to all of El Charro's employees, past and present.

Cariñosamente,
Carlotta

✦ ✦ ✦ ✦ ✦ ✦ ✦ ✦ ✦

| | |
|---|---|
| Publishers: | Bill Fisher, Howard W. Fisher and Helen V. Fisher |
| Editors: | Susan Lyons Anderson and Helen V. Fisher |
| Assistant Editor: | Candace Felice Flores |
| Managing Editor: | Sarah Trotta |
| Production Manager: | Deanie Wood |
| Cover & Book Design: | Fifth Street Design, Berkeley, California |
| Food Photography: | Lois Frank Photography, Santa Fe, New Mexico |
| Additional Photography: | Fifth Street Design |
| Published by: | Fisher Books is a member of the Perseus Books Group. www.perseusbooks.com |

**Library of Congress Cataloging-in-Publication Data**

Flores, Carlotta Dunn, 1946-
    El Charro Café: the tastes and traditions of Tucson / Carlotta
Dunn Flores.
        p.  cm.
    Includes index.
    ISBN 1-55561-121-4
    1. Cookery, Mexican.  2.  Cookery—Arizona—Tucson.  3. Charro
Café.   I. Title.
TX716.M4F58   1998                                    98-27325
641.5972—dc21                                          CIP

Printed in U.S.A.                                      Printing 5 4 3

# Contents

## Introduction / Introducción

## Recipes / Recetas

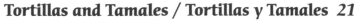

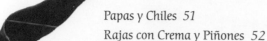

## Sauces / Salsas  59

## Meats, Poultry and Fish / Carnes, Pollo y Pescado  67

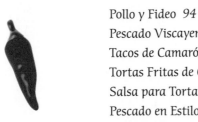

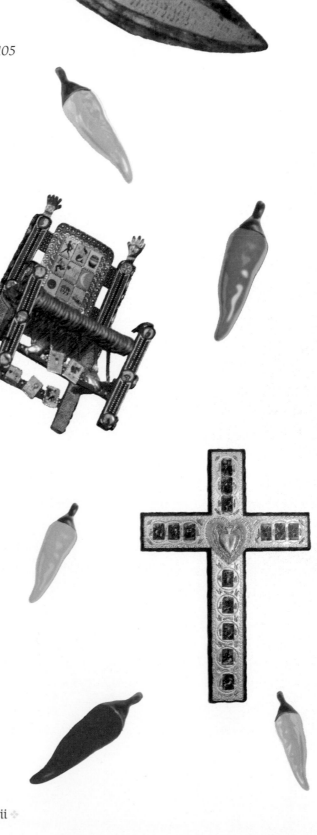

# Acknowledgments

W hen I was coaxing out this book I realized that I could not separate the recipes from my heritage—my memories of family, ancient and present.

✦ ✦ ✦ ✦ ✦

The stories and recipes I put together over the years involve my heritage and family traditions.
In this book I acknowledge and celebrate the blend of many nationalities in my family and in those of my neighbors and friends in my place of birth, Tucson, Arizona: Travelers from France, Spain and England, the indigenous peoples of Mexico, the Irish and Scots make me and my extended family the people we are today. I have written a tribute to my ancestors, and a legacy to the younger generations of our family. I hope it is a story they will be proud to "come home to" and hand on to their children.

**Monica holding baby Carlotta**

✦ ✦ ✦ ✦

Special thanks to Susan Lyons Anderson, Martin Fontes, Connie Martinez, Rafael Martinez, Francisco Norzagay, David Tineo, Borderlands Trading Company, Magellan Trading, Albaro Leon, Ron Genta, M. Gonzalo, Jose Galvez, and the memory of Monica and her El Charro.

# Introduction
## Introducción

# El Charro Café

*Growing up in Tucson, I was always fascinated by the history of the settlement that is fondly called the* Old Pueblo. *It includes stone-age peoples, early native inhabitants, Spanish explorers, padres and their missions, Apache raids, stone churches—and Mexican restaurants like our El Charro.* 🌶

### El Charro is Tucson

The El Charro story began with my great-grandfather, Jules Flin, a stocky young Frenchman and master stonemason. Shortly after arriving in Tucson in the 1860s, Monsieur Flin found himself toiling with chisel and hammer under the ceaseless

The Flin sisters, left to right clockwise: Louise, Francisca, Lydia and Monica, about 1916.

desert sun. He had been hired to create the stone façade for Tucson's San Agustín Church. (The façade still exists—now it graces the entrance of the Arizona Historical Society in Tucson.)

It was Flin's daughter, Monica, who began El Charro Café.

Jules married Carlota Brunet, also of French stock, in 1884. They spoke French throughout their lives, bringing up eight bilingual, then trilingual, children: Monica, Louise, Francisca, Lydia, Julio, Carlos, Stéphano and Agustín.

### Court Street Location

In the late 1890s, Flin built a sturdy home on Court Street, part of the exclusive residential section of Tucson known as *Snob Hollow.* Snob Hollow lay just outside the area that had encompassed the early Spanish *presidio.* The house was willed to Monica and is the fourth and present site of El Charro Café. It is designated Site Number 14 in El Presidio District on the National Register of Historic Places.

The high-ceilinged house is made of the black volcanic basalt rock that characterized most of Flin's buildings. He quarried the rock from his claim at the foot of "A" Mountain, just west of downtown.

### Monica

**El hambre hace salir al lobo de la cueva.**
**—Hunger makes the wolf leave his cave.**

My great-aunt, Monica Flin, remembered this as one of her father's favorite sayings. The culinary skills she learned in childhood were to afford her a high-profile life as one of Tucson's first businesswomen from the day she opened El Charro Café in 1922.

As a young woman, Monica had married and lived in Mexico. When her second husband died, she returned home to Tucson.

Four-year-old Carlotta with great-aunt Monica Flin.

Borrowing money from a sister, she opened a narrow, one-room restaurant and named it El Charro Café, after the romantic "gentlemen horsemen" known as *los charros* of Mexico.

### "No Service for Less Than 10 Cents"

In those early days, Monica worked on short-term credit. *Very* short-term. When a customer arrived, she would dash out the back door and cajole the neighboring Chinese grocer into giving her the provisions she needed. Then she would rush back to her kitchen, prepare the meal, serve it, collect the customer's money and return to the grocer to pay her bill. Somewhere there must have been a profit. Early menus from the 1920s show combination plates costing fifteen cents and a line that reads, "No service for less than 10 cents."

*The third El Charro, located on West Broadway, Tucson's main street in 1937.*

*A festive group posing in front of El Charro on July 4, 1954.*

After a few years, Monica moved her operation to Scott Street, into the graceful Temple of Music and Art (now home of the Arizona Theatre Company), and expanded it. But the Depression was hard on El Charro and most Tucson businesses.

Faced with a financial dilemma, Monica again turned to family. Her sister Francisca had a large building on West Broadway, the main street at the time, where she and her husband operated a drug store. One part was rented to a Chinese merchant, but other quarters were vacant and perfect for the new El Charro.

In 1968, Monica moved El Charro to the old family home on Court Street she had inherited, where it stands today. She brought with her the curios, tables and chairs, Mexican picture calendars, murals and saints' pictures (which make up most of our decor today) and most of her employees. She also brought along her father's rifles, which he had used to protect his family against Apaches, and mounted them above the new entrance.

By the early 1970s, Monica's health began to decline. In 1972, Monica let my mother, Zarina, take over. Then my husband, Ray, and I stepped in. We felt the

old restaurant could be made into a more modern and comfortable establishment. So the work began. Thus, El Charro is the oldest restaurant in the territory under continuous family ownership.

Now, with expansion to an East Broadway location and to the airport, our restaurants have undergone a new era of growth. Our catering business, Cocina Charro®, is proud to offer "Carlotta's

Cocina," cooking classes with me under Monica's divine guidance. Chonita Foods, our newest project, offers wholesale foods nationally.

One of Monica's favorite sayings was, "Whatever the meal, whatever the season, every meal at El Charro is served with color, music and, whenever possible, good company." It is a tradition that is still carried on at El Charro today.

★ ★ ★ ★ ★ ★ ★ ★ ★ ★ ★ ★ ★ ★ ★ ★ ★ ★ ★

## The Celebrities Always Came

El Charro has always been what is called a *movie-star restaurant.* When Hollywood film studios at Old Tucson were in their heyday in the 1940s, El Charro was a "must" dining experience for cowboys, cowgirls, good guys and bad, producers and directors ... who were always treated like family, just like the locals.

It is rumored that in her prime, Monica would sit out on the El Charro patio and sip martinis from teacups (a custom of hers left over from Prohibition), playing cards with John Wayne, in town to film Westerns at the Old Tucson studios. (Whether Wayne actually played cards, we don't know.) Wayne was a frequent dinner guest at El Charro, as were most of the actors who were being filmed in movies set around Tucson, including a young actor named Ronald Reagan.

Today, author, sociologist and Catholic priest Andrew Greeley is a regular guest and a special fan of our green corn tamales. He is dear to our heart. El Charro's cuisine and even our family dog, Rex, have been mentioned in his novels.

★ ★ ★ ★ ★ ★ ★ ★ ★ ★ ★ ★ ★ ★ ★ ★ ★ ★ ★

# Ingredients

## *Ingredientes*

*The Mexican food we enjoy in Tucson today is a unique cuisine not found in any other border town. Although you may recognize the names of some dishes—tacos, tamales, enchiladas, burros, chimichangas, chile colorado—our way of preparing them is different from anywhere else in the world.*

*Here in the very south of Arizona and the very north of Mexico, a wonderful mix of cultures came about as people moved from the heart of what had become Mexico to the arid north.*

*By the 1700s and 1800s the native ways of central Mexico had been well-infused with European cultures to become a whole new culture—Mexican. These people brought north with them different ideas about food. By necessity, they modified their diets by using foods of the Piman Indians of Sonora.*

*The families who were in the Tucson area before the Gadsden Purchase in 1853 put down roots and stayed. They intermarried with neighboring families, so the food did not change. In Tucson, we do not have the blend of Hispanic cultures that New York and Los Angeles have, or even Phoenix. So until recently, our food remained pure for generations.*

## The Foods of El Charro

*Haz todo con amor—*
**Do everything with love.**

That includes cooking!

Like Mexican cuisine itself, the language used to describe Mexican foods comes from many sources. **Azúcar** and **arroz** are from Arabic, a holdover from 700 years of Moorish rule in Spain prior to the conquest of the Americas. Native "Indians" taught the Spanish invaders words for the new foods they encountered.

The red (and green) pepper, for example, was altogether new to **los conquistadores**, so they adopted the Aztec's **Náhuatl** word for it, **chil**. French, German and English speakers who came much later— especially today's tourists, business partners and neighbors from the United States—also have added their words to the flexible and ever-changing Mexican-Spanish language.

In Tucson, you will not be called upon to speak Spanish unless you want to. Many people want to try. To help our patrons with terms that may be unfamiliar, I have created a glossary, like the one on page 131, which appears on the menu in our restaurants.

Enjoy! And come to see us in the Old Pueblo. We will make you **bienvenidos**, welcome.

# The Tortilla

At about the time of the northern migration from Mexico, something strange happened in the Tucson area. Corn, which had been the staple grain in the Sonoran Desert, as it was throughout the Americas, was supplanted by wheat. Europeans introduced fruits and livestock that were eagerly adopted by the indigenous peoples.

In the northern part of Mexico, where the diet was meager, there was a greater willingness to adopt the new ways of the Europeans than in the southern part, where variety in the diet was already great.

In Tucson, wheat (*trigo*) made the biggest impact. Wheat thrived in the mild Tucson winter. Farmers found they could grow two crops of wheat per year instead of just one for corn. So, while elsewhere in the New World corn remained king, Tucson became the hometown of the "flour" tortilla.

As irrigation improved, corn regained its place as a Tucson staple, and today a corn tortilla is as popular as a wheat-flour tortilla. In Tucson, unlike other regions with Mexican food, "tortilla" does not automatically mean a corn tortilla. If you want corn tortillas or flour tortillas, you have to specify. (Tortillas, page 25.)

## Nixtamal

To turn corn into tortillas requires several steps. First you have to turn the corn into hominy. Then you have turn it into *nixtamal*—corn mush or *masa*.

Hominy is corn that has been dried, husked and shelled, soaked in dolomitic lime water until the hulls can be rubbed off, and then stewed and rinsed. Hominy is used whole in *menudo*, a soup made with tripe and served as a hangover curative New Year's Day, and in *posole*, another soup made from hominy, whole beans and, traditionally, oxtails. (Posole, without oxtails, page 41.)

......................................................

**NOTITA:** *Canned whole hominy can be used in soups, but it cannot be turned into masa.*

......................................................

When hominy is ground, it becomes nixtamal and is shaped into corn tortillas (a nearly fat-free food) or mixed with lard (originally armadillo fat) and slathered on dried corn husks as the basis of the ancient *tamal*. (Tamales, page 28.)

Strictly speaking, both corn and wheat are called *harina* when ground. But through common use and corruption we in the Southwest mean wheat flour when we say *harina*. Thus *tortilla de harina* always means wheat-flour tortillas, or just flour tortillas. Its brother is called a corn tortilla or *tortilla de maiz*.

## The Sweet Corn of Summer

Fresh corn is part of summer life in Tucson when green corn tamale season rolls in with the late-summer monsoons. For these delicacies, young, white, sweet corn is scraped from cobs to become fresh corn masa. The masa is incorporated with cheese and chiles and steamed, wrapped in pale-green corn *hojas* (husks). (Green Corn Tamales, page 33.)

# Chile

Chiles, native to the Americas, have a long history in the culinary world. Anthropologists have unearthed 2000-year-old Peruvian pottery decorated with drawings of chiles. Christopher Columbus ate chiles on his first tour of the New World.

## The Anglo and the Chile

Chiles seem to inspire awe in those who eat them and those who watch others eat them. A Jesuit, Father Pfefferkorn, who followed the Jesuit Eusebio Francisco Kino into Arizona, developed a flaming passion for the chile—from a distance. He wrote of those who relished the chile: "They eat it with such appetite that their mouths froth and tears come to their eyes."

## A Wealth of Chiles

Tales of blistering Mexican food amuse, but take for granted that all Mexican food is hot—*picante. No es verdad*—It's not true, as you will see when you try the recipes in this book. Nevertheless, a hot chile is a joy.

There are 300 varieties of peppers, some scorching (*muy picante),* some mellow (*poco picante*). In the early days of El Charro, there were simply red chiles, green chiles and *chiltepínes,* the tiniest and hottest of them all, readily available in bulk.

Monica took whatever was brought to her. I am more selective with my chiles because I have the resources to get what I think is best. The intensity of peppers varies from batch to batch, from year to year and according to where the chiles were grown, so I do a lot of tasting to ensure I get exactly what I want.

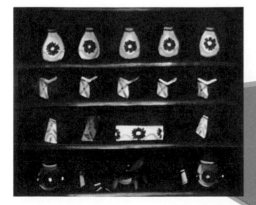

# Know Your Chiles

Chiles are as complicated as you want to make them. No exact science was used to name the varieties originally. Chile users resolutely stick by their own time-honored regional names. Therefore you'll find what looks just like the *poblano* chile you bought at one store called a *pasilla* or *ancho* in another; a long green chile may be called an *Anaheim* or even *Big Jim.* Modern grocers confuse the issue further because they are unfamiliar with chiles, and so even in Tucson you will find California- or Utah-based supermarket chains sticking a sign saying "pasillas" on the bin clearly holding poblanos.

Volumes are written about the chile. Most of what I have read, however, refers to these incongruities without much hope of clarification. They always end with the comment that no two chiles are alike anyway.

Our discussion of chiles here is confined to what I use in the restaurant and at home most often.

## Green chile

This category includes hundreds of varieties, ranging from pale green to black-green. The ones you'll see most often in supermarkets are the long green, or Anaheim, chiles. They are bright, fresh green, 4 to 7 inches in length, and taper gracefully if irregularly from about an inch-and-a-half wide at the stem to a somewhat blunted point. Usually they are considered mild. These are roasted and peeled (see instructions, page 10), then stuffed or chopped for adding to meat and vegetable stews. They are canned commercially, but canned chiles lose their inviting color.

The first choice among green chiles for stuffing is the poblano, called *ancho* (wide) because it is more squat (and holds more filling) than the long green, has a richer flavor and is a subtle black-green color when raw and fresh.

Jalapeños are favorites at the ballpark, usually pickled and canned, sliced and sprinkled on corn chips and blanketed with melted cheese. (See Los Chachos, page 18). Well, we have other ways with the jalapeño. A red-ripened jalapeño can be smoke-roasted. Once you have tasted the smoky flavor of this *chipotle,* you'll always remember it.

Two-inch long golden chiles are called *serranos.* They begin life green, change to orange and finally turn a lemony yellow. They are hotter than jalapeños.

## Red chile

This category includes almost any green chile that has been allowed to ripen fully. And during the drying process most chiles turn black-red, sometimes more black than red.

When the Anaheim chiles turn red, they are dried and strung into *ristras* or *sartas*, long bunches of them. (Many a beautiful sarta decorates front doors in Tucson, never to be eaten.) When boiled and mashed they are the basis for the mother of red chile sauces—Salsa de Chile Colorado or Chile Adobo (page 63).

The tiniest chile we use is the mighty chiltepín. These grow on small bushes (often used as ornamentals in Southwestern landscaping). The chiles, red like holly berries, add delight to a garden and fire to a sauce.

Many other chiles are available. There is no reason not to experiment with other varieties you encounter in markets. Rule of thumb: If the chile is small, it's hot!

## Green Chile Preparation

Chiles, especially the long green or Anaheim chiles, are usually prepared for cooking before they are incorporated into a recipe. In this book, you will be asked to prepare the chiles according to the following instructions.

The outer layer or skin of the chile and usually the seeds are removed before the chile is used. Cooks have devised several methods for doing this.

One method is to scorch the skin by holding the chile near a flame, such as under (or over) a gas broiler or stuck on a long fork held over the range-top burner. Others prefer to boil the chiles in oil until the skin loosens. Whichever way you choose, *¡cuidado!* Be careful! Never touch your eyes or mouth while you have chile oils on your hands. They are very potent. Wear plastic gloves if you find your skin is intolerant, and wash your hands well afterward.

**Direct-flame method:** Pierce chiles 2 or 3 times each with a fork and place them on your oven rack under the broiler. (Gas flames work better than electric burners.) Keep turning them until the chiles brown or blacken evenly. Immediately place them in a paper bag or covered pot and let them rest for about 20 minutes. When cool enough to handle, gently peel away most of the fragile, filmy skin, leaving the stem intact, if possible. The presence of the stem proves you are not serving canned chiles when you present Chiles Rellenos (page 57).

**Boiling-oil method:** Pierce each chile 2 or 3 times with a fork. Heat oil in a mini-fryer according to manufacturer's directions for French fries; or partially fill (about 1/3 of capacity) a deep, heavy saucepan with oil, and heat until the thermometer reaches the temperature marked for deep frying. Immerse the chiles, 2 or 3 at a time, into the oil until blisters form on the chiles. (The moisture in the chiles is considerable; expect much spattering while they are in the hot oil.) Immediately remove the chiles and submerge them in a bowl of cold water. When all chiles are blistered and cooled, peel them.

# Cactus, Fruits & Vegetables

Yes, edible cactus. The *nopales* (pads or ears) from the prickly-pear cactus in early spring are the most widely used culinary cactus in Tucson. We gather them from our yards or buy them already de-thorned in the supermarket. (Wild cacti are protected from poachers—and picklers, bakers and broilers—with strict laws that forbid the harming or gathering of plants.)

Don't be fooled when you see nimble little birds landing incautiously on the prickly pear and other spiny cacti. The spines hurt if not handled carefully. Wear gardening gloves and use tongs when scraping off the thorns, some of which are so fine you cannot see them with the naked eye.

Later in the spring, around Easter, the prickly pear bears egg-shaped *tunas,* fruit, in iridescent purple, lavender, cherry red, deep pink and pale pink, as well as marvelous tones of orange and yellow. Beautiful! And delicious. These too are handled with care, gloves and tongs. The Tohono O'odham, Tucson's native people, taught us to blanch, peel and purée them with sugar to make a syrup or a jelly. The tunas have natural pectin and make a jewel-like confection.

*Nopales* require quite a lot of preparation before they can be used in a recipe. Fortunately they are prepared commercially and are relatively easy to find in large supermarkets.

## Onion

I choose white onions for lots of dishes because I like the flavor, which usually is less bitter than that of Spanish or yellow onions. I've always called red onions "purple onions" and use them raw; when cooked, they turn a hideous color. Scallions or green onions are great as garnish or mixed into salsas.

## Vegetarian Dishes

Mexican food in general fits easily into the lives of vegetarians, since the cuisine was essentially meatless originally. Vegetarians, especially those who include cheese and eggs in their diets, are unfailingly pleased with the many dishes we put together on combination plates for them at our restaurants.

## Avocado

This has to be one of the most luscious of God's creations. It's buttery and smooth and turns any dish it graces into something special. The recipe lingo talks about peeling avocados. Actually it's usually easier to cut the fruit in half, lift out the big pit and scoop out the pulp from the skin. (For perfect slices, however, it *is* better to peel the skin first.) Avocados have a lot of calories and are used sparingly by dietary-oil-conscious people. Although avocados are high in calories and fat, they yield a "good" oil. As with everything else, let moderation be your guide when using avocados.

## Autumn Vegetables

Fall vegetables, such as squash and pumpkin, cater to Mexican food's Indian roots. These two vegetables in particular have added a distinctive charm and flavor to many of our tamales, salsas and side dishes. *Calabacitas*—a delicious medley of squash, corn, onion, garlic and Mexican white cheese—has long been a staple in Mexican homes.

# Beans and Rice

Nutritionists tell us the amount of protein we need in order to stay healthy is small and can be obtained not only by eating meat but by combining a grain with a legume—corn or rice with beans, for example. For vitamin A? Squash. Vitamin C? Chiles. *¡Es todo!*

At El Charro we use several kinds of beans. The *frijol* of choice, however, is the sturdy pinto bean. It gets its name (pinto means *paint* or *painted*) because, like the pinto pony, the bean is speckled, brown on brown. When cooked, it loses that mottled look and turns an even, inviting cowhide brown.

Rice, that versatile, easily stored and nutritious grain, came to the New World in the 1500s with the Europeans. In Tucson, which was not immediately affected by *los conquistadores* and their innovations, rice seems to have taken hold when the Chinese showed us how to cook it. At least that was the case in my family.

### Rice and the Chinese

When Monica was establishing El Charro in the 1920s, she, like other Tucsonans, depended heavily upon the region's Chinese settlers. These families, truck farmers and grocers in the beginning, continue to be important citizens of Tucson. Most Chinese arrived in the Southwest during the 1880s to work on the railroad that was linking the two coasts. When the Chinese laborers decided to stay, they sent to China for family, and many established themselves on leased land along the Santa Cruz River. They cultivated a wide variety of fruits and vegetables. Soon Chinese gardens and truck farmers were the envy of the agricultural community. It was logical that some of these successful farmers would open grocery stores in downtown Tucson.

The Chinese also influenced Mexican culture and food at that time through their employment in *las casas grandes* as servants and cooks. One of my dad's favorite dishes, rice with fried bananas, came from the Asian chef his family employed in Mexico. We continue to enjoy that recipe (page 47).

## Potatoes

Potatoes, a New World staple that found its way around the globe, are considered more than just a starch in Mexican cooking. They usually are treated as vegetables. They are used as a meat stretcher, incorporated into stews and soups, *sopas secas* (page 46) and in chunky sauces that accompany meat or fish.

### Garlic Purée

Whenever you see "garlic purée" in recipes in this book, the recipe calls for garlic prepared in the manner described below. If you use a lot of garlic, prepare a batch to be used within about a week's time. (Caution: Garlic spoils and can become toxic if stored in oil.)

To make about 1/2 cup of garlic purée, peel four whole heads of garlic by smashing the cloves with the side of a wide knife; the peels will slip off easily. Put the peeled garlic in a blender with about 1/4 cup of water, and purée. The purée should be about the consistency of applesauce. Store in a tightly closed glass jar in the refrigerator and use within a week.

Sometimes a recipe specifies that whole cloves or a head of garlic are to be used. This is usually so you can remove the garlic pieces before serving.

## Garlic

Garlic, called *ajo* in Spanish, is a primary ingredient in Mexican cuisine. It's so important, Arizona named a town Ajo. Adjust the amount called for in recipes to your personal taste.

## Cheese

You will notice an abundance of cheese in the recipes in this book.

Yellow cheese (yellow because it is dyed) is popular in U.S. Mexican food. At El Charro, we use a mild cheddar (longhorn or Colby cheddar) in some dishes, particularly for Tostada Grande (page 18), because it is pretty and melts well.

But don't neglect real Mexican cheese, which is in a class by itself. For several years we in the States could not get real Mexican cheese (because of pasteurization laws). When my first cookbook came out in 1989, I was obliged to combine several available cheeses to produce the quality I was looking for. In the book I called it *combination cheese*. It is a blend of cheddar, mozzarella and sometimes provolone (for a smoky, country taste) or feta (for sharpness). Combination cheese is still a viable substitute. Experiment. Have fun!

**NOTITA:** *Many fine Mexican cheeses are made with partially skimmed, rather than whole, milk.*

Mexican cheeses vary in texture from creamy to crumbly, and in taste from mild to sharp. Mexican cheese that is fresh (not aged) is called *queso fresco.* A few companies in the United States make 5-inch rounds of Mexican-style cheeses in several styles, even some flavored with jalapeño. The crumbly kind is *casero;* the best-melting is *panela.* Both are mild and creamy-white. An aged cheese, *cotija,* is salty and medium-hard. It crumbles when it is cut and keeps its shape somewhat when heated.

**NOTITA:** *In Mexico, cheese is a great luxury. On the counters in small grocery stores sits a thick wheel of white cheese, usually with a piece of damp cloth draped over to keep in moisture and keep out flies. Daily, homemakers or their niños buy a chunk of the cheese for cooking—or else just enough to stuff inside a folded corn tortilla for una merienda, a snack.*

# Herbs and Spices

*Orégano* is one of the most popular herbs used in the Mexican cooking of this region. Almost every home gardener has a an easy-to-grow plot of *orégano*. From those same gardens, we also enjoy *yerba buena* (the good weed, or mint), basil, thyme, sage, parsley and cilantro. Cinnamon (*canela*), cloves, nutmeg and other spices we usually buy whole and pulverize as we need them. Everyone has his or her own favorite dishes and varies them upon impulse, many times merely by changing the spicing. Although cumin (*comino*) is a common spice found in many versions of Mexican cuisine, I never use it, because it is not to my taste.

Ground chile—not commercial chili powder—is always available in Tucson supermarkets.

We make tea from *manzanilla* (chamomile), especially as a cure for colicky babies or to ease the labor of childbirth.

We value the tartness of lemon and limes and use them as we do spices or herbs. Lime juice in particular makes a healthful and satisfying salt substitute.

RESTAURANT
"EL CHARRO"
MONICA FLIN, PROP.

# Meats, Poultry & Fish

People who casually pick up a book on Mexican cuisine and scan the lists of ingredients can be excused for thinking, "It's all the same—tortillas, chiles, meat, cheese and beans!" But if they begin to look more earnestly, they are amazed at the variety of dishes that can be made from those few, basic ingredients. Western musicians, after all, create symphonies using but one scale with twelve notes.

Beef and pork have become mainstays in Mexican cuisine in the 400 years since they were imported. Stewed, roasted, boiled and shredded, broiled, ground, dried and flaked, grilled, spiced or plain, these meats, as well as the pervasive chicken, are the bases around which meals are created.

The coastal areas of Mexico always afforded abundant seafood. Tucson's nearest coastal town is Puerto Peñasco (Rocky Point) at the northernmost curve of the Sea of Cortés (the narrow body of water separating mainland Mexico from Baja California). Seafood was always prized and was imported to the desert early in Tucson's history. Natives fished mountain lakes and streams in the area. When refrigerated railroad cars were invented, fish was important cargo. As more and more Mexicans migrated to *El Norte,* fish recipes came with them.

The local love of seafood is still evident if you drive through the Mexican section of Tucson, with its myriad *marisco* stands dotting the streets. Nothing tastes better than a shrimp cocktail and an icy *cerveza* on a warm Tucson day.

## Pico de Gallo—A Seasoning Mix

A handy, all-purpose blend of spices to keep in a shaker on the dining table is *pico de gallo*—translated, the "bite from the rooster's beak."

I like to end meals that have been heavy on meat with a fresh fruit platter and pico de gallo. Pico de gallo is a dried chile, spice and salt mixture that brings out the best in fresh fruits. Sometimes I add a sprinkling of pecans or crumbled **queso fresco** over the fruit for an extra flavor boost.

This mixture can be used on almost any seasonal fruit, especially melons; but also on grapes, oranges, pears, kiwi, jicama, oranges, grapefruit, pears, plums and peaches. To my taste, strawberries are about the only significant exception. Even simpler (and one of my favorite snacks while hanging around the kitchen) is orange sections sprinkled with cinnamon.

For the family, I usually prepare about 3 pounds of chilled, assorted bite-size pieces of fruit arranged on a platter. When ready to serve the fruit, I sprinkle it with lime juice and the following seasoning:

### Pico de Gallo

A dusting of spices for fruit.

*3 tablespoons paprika*

*1 tablespoon cayenne pepper*

*1 tablespoon fine ground black pepper*

*1 tablespoon salt (decrease as desired)*

*2 tablespoons ground red chile*

Mix together and store in a shaker on your spice shelf.

# Recipes

## Recetas

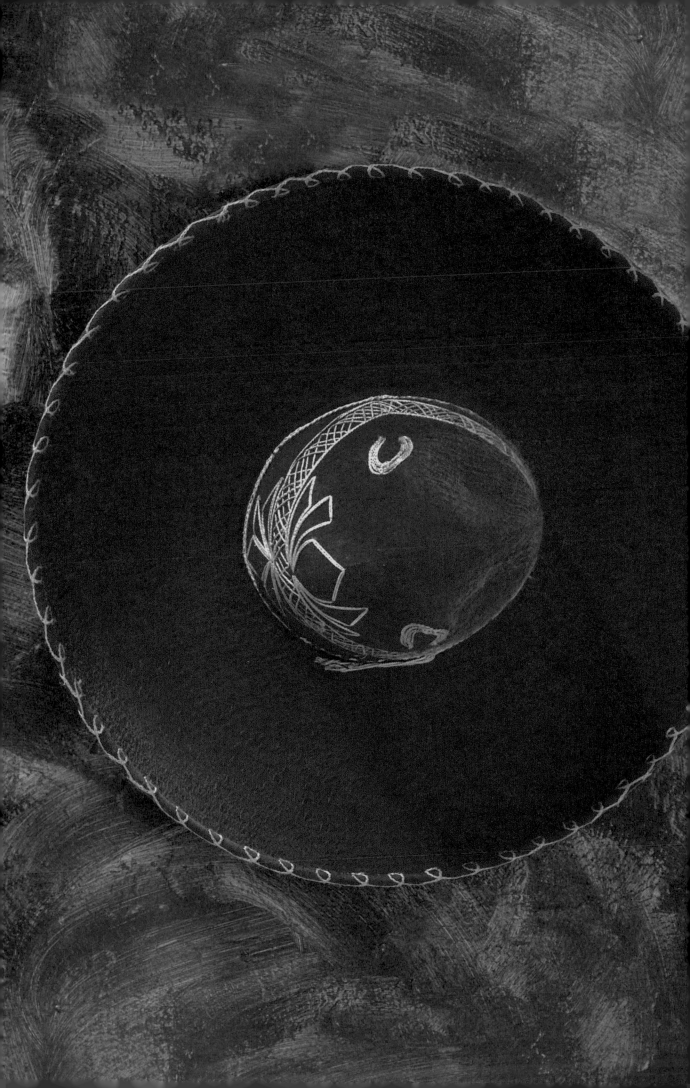

# Appetizers

## Antojitos

*Snack foods often are the first envoys of a cuisine to find a place on Americans' plates. Mexican snacks and appetizers include tacos and tostadas. At El Charro, most diners begin their meal with a cheese-laden El Tostada Grande and drinks.*

*The original tostadas were made simply by spreading tortillas with butter and baking them. This is still my favorite way. But over the years at El Charro we gradually added cheese and assorted toppings, including meat, chopped tomatoes, guacamole and onions. All or any of these, plus your imagination, can give you quite a taste treat.*

*The trick to ending up with a crisp tostada is to bake the unadorned tortilla in a 400°F (205°C) oven for a few minutes before adding any toppings. An exception to this rule: We sometimes spread a light layer of margarine or butter on them before baking if the tortillas are dry or stiff.*

*El Charro's tostadas are made with 18-inch flour tortillas, which are found only in the southernmost part of Arizona. One crisp at the restaurant is a main course for one person or an appetizer for 4 to 8 people. Eighteen-inch flour tortillas are difficult to find, even in Tucson supermarkets, but are available from tortilla factories here. Twelve-inch and 14-inch flour tortillas, however, are readily available in supermarkets nationwide for home use.*

# Tostada Grande de Tucson

*Original Large Cheese Crisp*

**Makes 4 to 8 appetizer servings**

*The custom is for each person to tear a piece from the tostada, although some people prefer to cut it into wedges, like pizza, before serving. A hot salsa is usually spooned onto each bite.*

**One (18-inch) flour tortilla**

**16 oz. longhorn cheese, shredded**

Bake tortilla 5 minutes directly on rack in oven preheated to 400°F (205°C). Remove tortilla from oven and place on pizza pan. Spread cheese evenly over the tortilla and bake until cheese is bubbly and completely melted, about 5 minutes. Serve on pizza tray or other round platter.

**NOTITA:** *At El Charro we use the larger 18-inch tortillas for our Tostada Grande. Smaller tortillas are good too; adjust the amount of cheese to suit.*

# Los Chachos

*Corn Tortilla Chips with Melted Cheese*

**Makes 6 to 8 servings**

*El Charro's version of nachos has to be . . . Chachos.*

**4 cups totopos (commercial or homemade corn chips, page 27)**

**16 oz. longhorn cheese, shredded**

**6 fresh Anaheim chiles, roasted, page 10, chopped**

**3 large tomatoes, chopped**

**GARNISH; CHOOSE FROM:**

**1 cup green olives, chopped**

**1 cup avocado chunks**

**Jalapeño rings**

**Chopped onions or scallions**

**Diced red or green bell pepper**

**Sour cream**

**Refried beans**

Arrange chips, overlapping slightly, on pizza pan or cookie sheet. Sprinkle evenly with cheese, chile and tomato. Bake at 400°F (205°C) 5 minutes, or until cheese melts. Garnish as desired before serving.

**NOTITA:** *The microwave speeds up the process, but does not develop flavors as well as baking in a conventional oven.*

# Quesadilla

*Mexican Grilled Cheese Sandwich*

**Makes 1 dozen**

*A favorite dinner at El Charro is a bowl of Carne Seca (page 72, Carne Seca Substitute) and a quesadilla with a side of guacamole (opposite page).*

**16 to 32 oz. panela or nonfat cheese, crumbled**

**12 (10-inch) flour tortillas**

**Oil or vegetable spray**

**OPTIONAL FILLINGS:**

**Fresh Anaheim or jalapeño chiles, roasted, page 10, diced**

**Chicken or beef, cooked and shredded**

Divide cheese and optional filling into 12 portions. Place one portion in center of first tortilla. Fold tortilla in half and flatten gently. Secure with wooden pick, if necessary. Repeat with remaining tortillas.

Lightly oil, or spray with vegetable oil, a large skillet. Place skillet over medium heat for 2 minutes, then place prepared tortilla on hot skillet and cook about 1 minute. Carefully flip the tortilla and cook the other side until brown.

Serve immediately. For easier handling, cut into wedges.

**NOTITA:** *Corn tortillas, with higher nutritional value and only a trace of fat, may be substituted for flour tortillas. The result is a totally different taste and appearance. My mother prefers her quesadillas this way: small, fresh corn tortillas with a smattering of Mexican white cheese grilled to tasty perfection.*

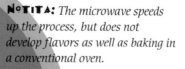

# Super Bowl Fundido con Sabores de Chiles

*Cheese Fondue with Chiles*

Makes 6 to 8 servings

*Fondue, or fundido, means a hot or melted food, usually cheese or chocolate, often with wine or liqueur added. Dip chips, cubes of cake or French bread, vegetable sticks or bite-size pieces of fruit into the hot mixture. This version is especially good to serve when the whole family gets together at home to watch a big event like the Super Bowl.*

$^{1}/_{2}$ **lb. feta-and-garlic cheese, crumbled**

$^{1}/_{2}$ **lb. processed jack-and-green chile cheese, shredded**

$^{1}/_{2}$ **lb. longhorn cheese, shredded**

$^{1}/_{2}$ **lb. Mexican cheese, crumbled**

**2 jalapeños, sliced into rings**

**1 chile chipotle, sliced into rings**

**1 fresh Anaheim chile, roasted, page 10, cut into rings**

**6 tablespoons Taco Sauce, page 64, or other salsa**

$^{1}/_{2}$ **cup chopped onion**

Coat a microwave dish with vegetable oil spray. Sprinkle grated cheeses in an even layer. Mix all chiles together and sprinkle on top, along with Taco Sauce or salsa of your choice. Microwave on high power until bubbly. Serve with your favorite chips or vegetables and with more salsa.

**NOTITA:** *Pour melted cheese mixture over individual servings of chips and top with chiles for a deluxe version of ballpark nachos.*

# Guacamole

*Avocado Dip*

Makes about 5 cups

*Contrary to culinary mythology, there really is no way to keep guacamole from turning brown. Make guacamole as close to serving time as possible. Serve in a lettuce cup, topped with red bell pepper strips.*

**4 large avocados, seeded, peeled and mashed**

**4 large tomatoes, diced**

$^{1}/_{2}$ **cup fresh Anaheim chiles, roasted, page 10, chopped**

$1^{1}/_{2}$ **teaspoons garlic salt**

**Pinch dried oregano**

$^{1}/_{4}$ **cup white onion, chopped**

**1 cup shredded longhorn cheese or other cheese**

Combine all ingredients in a nonreactive bowl, mixing well. Cover with plastic wrap and refrigerate until ready to serve. Serve with *totopos* (corn chips, page 27), or use as filling for a vegetarian Burro.

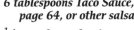

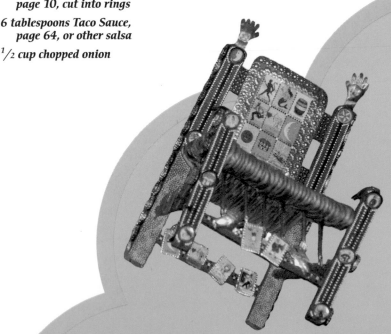

# Tortillas & Tamales
## Tortillas y Tamales

*Although few of us make our own tortillas these days, my respect for their lore and history demands that I at least explain how tortilla-making is done.*

*My childhood was filled with the sweet smell of masa. Masa is dough or mash, made from either wheat flour (harina) or ground dried corn.*

*Each masa has its own identity. Masa made of dried corn is the ancient masa, masa de elote or de maíz. When it is made from moist, fresh corn, it is called masa de elote fresca.*

*Wheat flour is comparatively new to our region. The Europeans brought wheat to the New World only in the sixteenth century. Ancient corn masa gets all the play in Southwest Nouvelle cuisine, especially in Santa Fe (where blue corn is king), Los Angeles and at a host of wonderful new restaurants in Tucson. This nueva masa is blended with red chile, green chile, mashed black beans, rich salsas and garlic, much the way pastas are being reinvented with flavoring additions.*

**Photo on pages 22-23: Masa, Tamales de Chile Colorado**

# Tortillas de Harina

## *Flour Tortillas*

**Makes about 2 dozen**

*Wrapped snugly, tortillas freeze well. They may be defrosted while still wrapped.*

**8 cups all-purpose flour**
**1 tablespoon salt**
**$^1/_2$ cup lard**
**$2^3/_4$ cups warm water**
**$^1/_4$ cup lard, additional**

In a large bowl, sift together flour and salt. Using hands, quickly blend the $^1/_2$ cup lard into flour mixture. Gradually add warm water, mixing constantly, until soft dough (not sticky) is obtained. Turn out on floured board and knead 10 minutes. Pat lightly with some of the additional lard, cover with a dish towel and set aside to rest 5 minutes.

Divide dough into about 24 pieces the size of tennis balls. Pat each ball with lard, cover with waxed paper and let rest 30 minutes.

Now to shape them: Traditionally, the flour tortilla is patted out by hand; however, a rolling pin may be used. Flour the board generously and roll dough into circles about 6 to 8 inches in diameter—or larger and thinner, if things are going well.

Meanwhile, heat the *comal* (or a large, heavy, well-seasoned griddle) to very hot. (It is hot enough when drops of water on it sizzle instantly.) Do *not* grease it.

Bake the tortillas on the *comal,* first one side, momentarily, until it bubbles slightly; then lift, flip and cook the other side. Tortillas will characteristically brown in the areas where the dough bubbled and remain white elsewhere. They can be held for a short time before serving wrapped well in foil or plastic. But eat them as soon as possible.

## There Was Some Confusion . . .

Not everybody in the world recognizes our large, thin flour tortillas right away. Alas, presidential hopeful Thomas E. Dewey didn't have the benefit of a tutor when he came to El Charro during his election campaign in 1946.

Dewey and his aides sat down to a table equipped with two saucers hiding a giant, folded tortilla. While lost in deep politician-talk, he apparently did not notice the small white napkin under his elbow, and nonchalantly unwrapped the warm, hanky-thin tortilla from beneath the saucer, unfolded it and tucked it neatly into his collar, in anticipation of a fine Mexican meal. No one had the nerve to tell him his error.

Monica put the Dewey Napkin on display, where it eventually dried up and blew away.

Mr. Dewey's mistake is understandable. An El Charro guest never sees a whole tortilla grande, spread open in all its silky glory (except covered with melted cheese as a Tostada Grande, page 18). We serve the tortilla folded, wrapped in a piece of white paper and placed between two saucers or in a basket to keep it warm. Seasoned diners know to quickly unwrap the paper, tear off a hunk of the tortilla and cover the remainder. They use the tortilla just like a piece of bread or a roll, sometimes to push a little food onto the fork or sometimes deliberately wrapping a forkful of food in the tortilla piece.

# Big Flour Tortillas

We take our overgrown flour tortillas for granted here. We are the only region in the world that makes tortillas 18 inches in diameter. Flour tortillas, besides being daily bread, are used for the choice cheese crisp (the quesadilla), burros, deep-fried chimichangas or dessert pastries, warmed and sprinkled with cinnamon and sugar.

That's the old way to make a sweet, or *dulce*, with flour tortillas. The nontraditional new ways with flour tortillas include peanut-butter-and-jelly burros in lunch boxes; tortillas wrapped around chocolate or mousse and topped with sweetened whipped cream; and tortillas folded around a mixture of chopped nuts and maple syrup.

# Basic Uses for Flour and Corn Tortillas

*Basic uses for flour and corn tortillas are described below. Refer to them when using one of the many vegetable, meat and fish fillings throughout this book.*

## Mastering the Burro

A burro, or burrito, is made by rolling a soft flour tortilla around a filling. It sounds simple, but there is an art to rolling the perfect burro. The tortilla (the bigger the better) must be very supple. Warming it helps.

To roll: Take a 10-, 12-, 14- or 18-inch tortilla, lay it out flat and fold up the bottom third to make a solid base, as if you were beginning to fold a letter. Spread filling on the solid base, then roll the base and filling one turn up, so that the fold is in the center and widest part of the tortilla. Now fold in each side of the tortilla and roll again, once or twice, until you have a neat package. Place seam side down for serving.

A *burro* is made with 14- to 18-inch tortillas. A *burrito* is made with smaller tortillas. At El Charro, we only serve burros.

## Chimichanga: Deep-Fried Burro

When flour tortillas are deep fried, they puff and brown, almost like puff pastry, because of the shortening they contain. "Thingamajig" is about as close as anybody has come to a translation for *chimichanga*, an El Charro invention.

To prepare a chimichanga, follow the same preparation and rolling technique as for the burro, but fasten the seam with wooden picks. Stuff with various meat- or poultry-filling preparations (see pages 82, 83, 88) and deep-fry in a large pot or deep fryer filled one-third full of hot oil (360°F or 180°C), until it is golden brown on all sides.

Use tongs to remove the browned chimis and drain them on a thick layer of paper towels. Keep them warm until ready to serve. Remove the wooden picks before serving. Let guests garnish their own with enchilada sauce, shredded cheese, lettuce, avocado slices, sour cream and salsa.

With the cocktail party came the Lilliputian version of chimichangas—the mini chimis. Use the smallest available flour tortillas for these, of course. Or use large tortillas, cutting them into four or six pieces to make the mini chimis. Mini chimis are best served immediately after frying.

## Corn Masa

When nixtamal (processed corn, page 8) is ground, it becomes fresh masa dough, which is spread on *hojas* (dried corn husks) to make tamales. The messy procedure has led many of us to buy our masa already prepared from tortilla factories or Mexican markets. Supermarkets all over Tucson and other cities with Mexican populations carry fresh masa during the Christmas season, when tamale-making is traditional.

Usually corn tortillas are made by rolling, not patting. Unlike the glutinous wheat-flour mixture, masa is not elastic.

Buy some masa and practice. If you can't find fresh masa, buy dry Quaker® Masa and follow the directions on the box. It's fun and made easier by using a tortilla press.

When flattened slightly into 5- or 6-inch circles, corn masa becomes *gorditas* for Enchiladas Sonorenses (flat enchiladas) or Chalupas (page 27), savory tart shells made of masa that include cooked, mashed potato.

Baked or deep-fried, thinner corn tortillas harden into flat tostada bases or U-shaped taco shells.

Corn tortillas are also used as chips (*Totopos*) or crisp strips, which I call *Totopitos* (page 27). The triangular chips are used for dips; the 1-inch by $1/4$-inch strips are found, like croutons, in soups or as the topping for salads.

## Tacos

Tacos are made with corn tortillas filled with meat, vegetables, fish or beans and topped with shredded cheese, lettuce or cabbage, diced tomato and a chile salsa. Some prefer to form the shells first by lightly frying the tortilla until crisp; others fill the tortilla, roll and secure with a wooden pick, and then fry it, garnishing after that.

## Tostada: the Flat Taco

A *tostada,* often served as an appetizer in Mexican restaurants in Tucson, could be described as a taco left flat. The toasted (fried) tortilla is the base under a decorous display of meat, beans and toppings. Tostadas can be dainty tidbits or whopping platefuls.

## Enchiladas

Enchiladas are soft corn tortillas filled with any number of imaginative combinations, not just cheese. Some of our favorite fillings are carne seca; a medley of vegetables including potatoes, carrots, squash and onions, creamed spinach, shredded, cooked chicken breast, or sautéed mushrooms. After rolling tortillas around the filling, place seam side down in a baking dish. Pour a sauce over them, sprinkle with shredded cheese, and bake until bubbling. Serve topped with sour cream and Guacamole (page 19) if desired. A smooth green sauce is sometimes served warm on enchiladas (page 65).

*Enchiladas Sonorenses* (Sonoran-style enchiladas), like Chalupas, are not rolled (page 27).

## Gordita

These days my favorite tortilla forms are called *gorditas*—little fatsos—which can be made from dry corn masa or wheat flour. They can be eaten alone like bread, or filled with something good. They are not rolled or pressed as thinly as regulation tortillas, so they hold up well under hearty toppings.

## Chalupas

Chalupas deserve a class by themselves. I believe they must be the oldest kind of tortillas, just because they are so simple, unrefined—and good.

For these, the masa includes a small amount of grated, cooked potato. A ball of masa is patted out into the shape of a canoe (*chalupa*) or a tart, and the edge is pinched so the filling stays in place.

# Totopos y Totopitos

## Corn Chips and Strips

**12 corn tortillas**
**2 cups vegetable oil**

Heat oil in heavy 7-inch skillet or saucepan. Cut corn tortillas with scissors to desired shapes and fry briefly in hot oil, a few at a time. Drain on paper toweling, cool and bag. Use within a day or two.

**LOW-FAT NOTITA:** *A healthy alternative to the fried chip is the baked corn chip. Cut tortillas to desired shape and bake on a tray at 350°F (175°C) for approximately 8 minutes or until edges of tortilla pieces begin to brown. Turn over the pieces and continue baking to desired crispness. Remove from oven and sprinkle lightly with salt. Serve immediately.*

# Enchiladas Sonorenses

## Flat Corn Masa Patties with Red Chile Sauce

#### Makes 6 to 8 servings

*This is the basic masa shell, wonderful with a little sauce, cheese and cabbage or lettuce. Like tacos or tostadas, it can carry any of the beef, pork, poultry, fish or vegetable fillings offered elsewhere in this book. Then it is called a chalupa.*

**2 lb. fresh corn masa**
**1 teaspoon salt**
**$1/2$ teaspoon baking soda**
**1 medium potato, cooked and grated (for fluffiness)**
**$1/2$ cup shredded cheddar cheese**
**Oil for frying**

GARNISH:

**4 cups Salsa de Chile Colorado, page 63**
**1 cup sliced green olives**
**1 cup chopped green onions**
**1 cup shredded longhorn cheese, or other cheese**
**Sliced radish**
**Lime slice**
**1 oz. vinegar**
**1 tablespoon dried oregano**
**1 or 2 heads iceberg lettuce (or 1 head green cabbage), shredded**

Mix masa, salt, soda, potato and cheese. Shape into balls the size of an egg. Place, one at a time, between two sheets of wax paper and flatten with a rolling pin or tortilla press to 4 or 5 inches in diameter, or $1/4$ inch thick, whichever you arrive at first. Make these ahead and cover with damp paper towels.

Heat 1 inch of oil in small skillet and fry each patty 5 minutes on each side and drain on paper towels.

To garnish: Cover each patty with hot Salsa de Chile Colorado (page 63) and top with olives, onion and cheese. Mix the vinegar and dried oregano in a small bowl and serve on the side with a bowl of shredded lettuce or cabbage.

**Chalupa variation:** To shape masa for a chalupa shell, see page 26. Try Picadillo (page 79) as a filling.

## Bocaditos

Just as we are taught not to butter a whole piece of bread but to break off a small piece first, so it is with tortillas. You are no longer a novice at eating Mexican food when you tear off a piece of tortilla to eat as a *bocadito*, little mouthful.

Spanish speakers, especially those who came to Spanish from *Náhuatl*, love to assign diminutives to everything they enjoy.

# Tamales

The ancient tamal is the most grand of all the corn masa creations. The masa is not rolled or patted, just smeared on corn husks and steamed.

The tamal and its cousins in cultures around the world are as old as the ground wherein they were steamed. To our family and our extended family, it is our history and tradition—not just meat and masa—that are wrapped in tamales. I recall the comfort of tamales at times of bereavement, at times of joy, at times of closeness with others. This ancient food holds memories good and sad—but most of all it contains our family identity.

Perhaps that is why I think of the tamal as the ultimate comfort food. At Christmas, tamales mean "you are welcome here with us to celebrate the birth of Christ." At home, they now are considered a party food, or a special-occasion dish, as our turkey is at Thanksgiving.

The most important role of Tamales de Chile Colorado (red tamales) occurs on Christmas Eve. Days in advance, families gather to prepare the tamales at parties known as *tamaladas*. It would not be Christmas Eve in a Mexican home without tamales. When visiting during the Christmas season, you expect to be served tamales. And of course, you too are expected to have a supply ready for company.

## Tamales Any Way You Like Them

There are at least 50 varieties of the ancient tamal that I know of. They include those made with meats and poultry cooked in red or green chile sauces, poached and shredded meat or poultry, and vegetable fillings.

The *tamal* (singular form of *tamales,* but commonly seen and pronounced *tamale*) also can be sweet, *Tamales de Dulce*. These have sugar added to the masa and can have combinations of almonds, candied fruits, preserves and even beans (cooked without the savory seasonings) and cinnamon. Sometimes pink coloring is added to distinguish sweet tamales from the savory kind.

I include a recipe for a sweet tamale on page 118.

## A Tamal for All Seasons

Tamales de Elote (Green Corn Tamales) are reserved for late summer and early fall, when the fresh green—or white or sweet—corn is at its best. The corn is shucked, and selected husks, *hojas*, are saved to be used as tamal wrappers.

**NOTITA:** *Here is another difference between the two main varieties of tamales. Red tamales are made in the winter, so their hojas (wrappers) have dried and must be softened in warm water for shaping. Green Corn Tamales are made in corn season, so their hojas are already moist and impart a mellow, grassy flavor to the summer tamales.*

## Tamales, Like Children, Need Your Time

The recipes for tamales I include in this book are detailed and may seem complicated. Well, they are. But they are not hard! (There *is* a difference.) The best way to learn to make tamales is to participate in a *tamalada*. Then you will appreciate why tamales are so special and why the whole family gets together for the task.

Making tamales is labor-intensive, not something to attempt if there is anything else you would rather be doing. The meat mixture for red tamales, however, can be prepared a day or two in advance.

★★★★★★★★★★★★★★★★★★★★★★★★★

## Tamal Tips

Here are a few tips to give you a boost.

★ Never cook tamales in an aluminum pot. Aluminum will give tamales an unpleasant taste. Also, do not put aluminum foil next to tamales when steaming. Instead, if necessary, place white freezer paper over tamales, **then** a layer of foil to make a tight seal on the steamer.

★ Green corn tamales should be made the same day the corn is ground or milled. Fresh, sweet corn is delicate and spoils quickly.

★ Green corn tamales can be frozen, but I do not like to do it. They seem to take on a hint of sourness. Red tamales do not change appreciably after freezing.

★★★★★★★★★★★★★★★★★★★★★★★★★

# Tamales de Chile Colorado

## Red Chile Tamales

**Makes 5 dozen**

*Every family I know has a story unique to its tamales. As families divide and scatter, these recipes have traveled with them.*

*Don't let the length of this recipe discourage you. I have included details that I hope will help, not confuse.*

**MEAT MIXTURE:**

*3 lb. roast of beef (brisket)*

*3 lb. roast of fresh pork (butt)*

*3 qt. water*

*1/4 cup garlic purée, page 12*

*1 tablespoon salt*

**SAUCE:**

*2 qt. water*

*1 lb. dried red chiles*

*3/4 cup vegetable shortening*

*3/4 cup flour*

*6 cups reserved broth*

**MASA DOUGH:**

*2 pkg. dried corn husks*

*1 3/4 lb. vegetable shortening*

*5 lb. corn masa*

*3 teaspoons salt*

*2 cups reserved broth*

*1/4 cup red chile purée (For instructions, see Sauce, below)*

*Green olives, with pits*

## Day One

In a 10-quart stock pot, place meat and water and bring to the boil. Skim off froth. Add garlic purée and salt. Reduce heat and simmer until meat is tender, skimming frequently. Remove meat; strain and reserve broth. Refrigerate broth. Shred meat, removing all fat, bone and gristle. Cover and refrigerate. When broth is chilled, remove and discard the fat.

## Sauce

Remove stems from chiles and place pods in a pot with water. Bring to the boil; simmer until pods soften. Strain and reserve broth. In blender, process chiles, a batch at a time, with a little broth until smooth. In a 10-quart stock pot, melt vegetable shortening. Whisk in flour to make a roux. Cook to golden brown. Heat 6 cups reserved meat broth and slowly whisk into roux. Add chile purée and simmer 20 minutes.

Stir shredded, cooked meat into sauce and simmer to blend seasonings. Taste and correct seasonings. Refrigerate.

**NOTITA:** *Can be prepared a day or two ahead up to this point.*

## Day Two

First soften corn husks in hot water for 10 minutes. Remove silk and clean the husks. Drain and cover with a damp towel.

Next, make masa dough. Beat the vegetable shortening, in batches, until very light and fluffy—the consistency of whipped cream. Place half the vegetable shortening in an electric mixer. Beat at least 10 minutes, until very soft and fluffy. Meanwhile bring 2 cups reserved broth to simmer. When the vegetable shortening is fully beaten, add half the masa and simmering broth, a spoonful at a time, beating constantly. Add half the salt and, if desired, fold in 1/4 cup chile purée for color. Remove to large bowl. Repeat with remaining ingredients.

To test the masa dough to see if it is fluffy enough, drop a pinch of dough into a glass of cold water. It is perfect if it floats.

## To Assemble:

(See illustration, page 33.) Open a large corn husk with the pointed end at the bottom. Spread 2 tablespoons of masa dough onto the husk to within 1 inch of its edges. Place 1 heaping tablespoon of meat filling and an olive in the center of the masa dough.

Tightly roll corn husk lengthwise around the filling. Fold the pointed end up. Repeat with remaining masa dough and filling. Place tamales, open end up, in the refrigerator or freezer 1 to 2 hours before steaming.

## To Steam:

Place tamales on a rack in a steamer (or improvise a steamer by resting a wire rack on clean stones, empty tuna cans or corn cobs in a Dutch oven or large kettle.) Add water to just below the rack. Arrange tamales, open end up, on rack. Bring water to the boil; cover, reduce heat and steam about 45 minutes. Add boiling water as necessary, but be sure the tamales do not sit in the water.

**NOTITA:** *Red tamales reheat well in the microwave oven, wrapped in damp paper towels, or in a conventional oven, wrapped in foil.*

**NOTITA:** *Tamales make a wonderful breakfast dish. Leave the steamed tamal in its husk and heat it in the oven until the husk is crispy. Open the husk and top with a fried egg.*

*Photo on pages 30-31: clockwise, from upper right—Tamales de Elote, Chalupa, Chimichanga enchilada style with Guacamole and sour cream cups*

## Making the Green Corn Tamal

I can't believe that after all these years there is no way but the old-fashioned way to make green corn tamales. Maybe that's a good thing. The labor involved in producing green corn tamales is mountainous—partly because you never want to make a skimpy batch.

First, the corn has to be just right. Green corn (actually the kernels are white in color) is at its peak in the southwestern United States in late summer. Everyone waits eagerly for the first signs of green corn.

Different families have different recipes for green corn tamales. Some are simple and sweet, relying on the delicacy of the corn mush to please as no other concoction ever could. Others like to jazz them up with lots of cheese (cottage cheese, Mexican white cheese, modern yellow cheese, such as longhorn), chiles (hot jalapeños or milder ancho or Anaheims) and other touches. A good amount of lard is traditional in green corn tamales. Some families today substitute vegetable shortening, as I do.

If you really do want to make a small batch of green corn tamales and don't live in an area with a tortilla factory to grind your corn masa for you, you certainly can use your food processor or hand-cranked meat grinder. For that matter, you could use a coarse mortar and pestle, as our ancestors did.

There are also specialized "de-kerneling" devices. A blade-edged ring is secured around the ear and pushed along the kernels, making quick work of dozens of ears of corn—once you get the hang of it. I have found that a comfortable, very sharp serrated knife does a good job, too. The most important caution—besides watching out for worms—is not to cut too deeply into the kernels. To do so would add bits of the tough cob, which are not bad for you, but can give the tamal a bitter taste.

32

# Tamales de Elote

## Green Corn Tamales

**Makes 5 dozen**

*"Green corns are here!" For generations, Tucsonans of all backgrounds have awaited that sign in El Charro's window. It means not only good eating, but also that the monsoons are here and, soon, relief from the desert heat.*

*Five dozen good-sized ears of green corn will yield at least 10 pounds of kernels—sometimes more. In Tucson, we can easily find all we need at fresh produce stands. You can take cut kernels to a tortilla factory for grinding, or grind them yourself in a sturdy blender or through a fine meat grinder.*

**5 dozen ears fresh white (green) corn**

**2¹/₂ lb. vegetable shortening**

**2 tablespoons salt**

**2 tablespoons sugar**

**2 lb. longhorn or Mexican cheese, shredded**

**2 cups cottage cheese**

**4 cups fresh Anaheim chiles, roasted, page 10, chopped**

GARNISH:

**2 cups Salsa de Tomatillo Cruda, page 62**

To remove husks from corn, cut 2 or 3 inches from the top, enough to barely cut off the tip of the cob and the corn silk; cut off the base of the cob to reach the kernel area. Slip off husks, rinse, drain and set aside.

Scrape the kernels from the cob with a knife, an electric knife or special tool for this purpose sold in some cookware shops. Be careful not to cut into the cob. Grind the corn in a blender or meat grinder (or, if possible, take the kernels to the tortilla factory and have them ground).

Immediately after grinding the kernels, use an electric mixer to whip the vegetable shortening and salt, in batches, until fluffy. Combine beaten shortening mixture and ground corn to form green-corn masa.

In another large bowl, combine salt, sugar, cheddar cheese, cottage cheese and chiles.

To make the tamales, the masa should be thick. Select the biggest husks for the tamales. Place 2 tablespoons masa in the center of one husk. Now place a tablespoonful of the cheese-and-chile mixture in the center of the masa.

Fold the left edge of the corn husk over to the right edge of the filling. Fold the right edge over the left. Fold up the bottom third of the husk and turn the tamal over to keep it intact. Place open end up in a pan. Repeat until the fillings are used up. Refrigerate or freeze to congeal, then wrap. Steam according to directions for Red Chile Tamales (page 29) and serve with Salsa de Tomatillo Cruda on the side.

**Assembling the tamal**

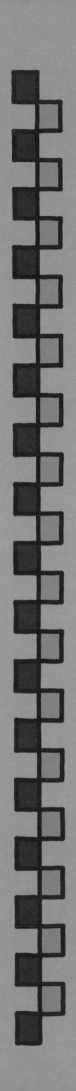

# Soups

## Sopas

*A delicious soup can cure all ills—heartbreak, a chill, illness or simple hunger. To be offered a bowl of homemade soup is to be offered a part of someone's soul.*

*A good, basic meat stock is made simply by simmering bones in water, perhaps with one or two carrots, celery ribs and onions, herbs or spices. Stocks usually are not served by themselves, but are the foundation of many a soup and sauce. At El Charro we do not add salt to the stock, but prefer to season the finished soup or sauce.*

*Make stock in a quantity large enough so you can use some right away and freeze the rest. First place two or three pounds of beef or chicken bones (or both) in a large stock pot. Fill the pot with cold water, bring to the boil, then immediately reduce heat.*

*Simmer uncovered for several hours, removing froth frequently. The longer it simmers and reduces, the richer the stock.*

*Cool, discard the bones and strain the stock to use in soups, enchilada sauce or in rice and pasta preparations.*

**Photo on pages 36-37: clockwise, from upper left—Sopa de Tomate, Albóndigas, Cocido, Caldo de Queso, Sopa de Tortilla**

# Caldo de Queso

## Cheese and Potato Soup

*Makes 6 to 8 servings*

*Rough-cut potatoes and stringy cheese make this a soul-satisfier. Puréed and topped with a spoonful of tomato salsa, it's elegant. Caldo de Queso may be refrigerated for use the next day or frozen for later use.*

**4 medium potatoes, peeled and cubed**

**5 cups water**

**3 cups beef stock**

**1 medium white onion, sliced and separated**

**1 teaspoon salt, or to taste**

**$^1/_2$ cup garlic purée, page 12**

**8 fresh Anaheim chiles, roasted, page 10, chopped**

**$1^1/_4$ cups milk or evaporated milk**

**2 large tomatoes, coarsely chopped**

**4 cups cubed or shredded longhorn cheese or crumbled Mexican cheese**

In an 8-quart stock pot, cook potatoes in water until soft. Remove potatoes with slotted spoon and set aside. Add beef stock to potato water and bring to the boil. Add salt, garlic purée, Anaheim chiles, onion and milk. Simmer 10 minutes. Taste and adjust seasoning, adding more chile, if you like. Add cooked potatoes and tomatoes and simmer about 10 minutes.

To serve: Place $^1/_2$ cup of cubed cheese in warm bowls and ladle soup over the cheese.

**LOW-FAT NOTITA:** *Low-fat or fat-free cheese and nonfat condensed milk make an acceptable, lighter soup.*

# Sopa de Tortilla

## Tortilla Soup

*Makes 6 servings*

*For a somewhat heartier soup, add one cup of cooked, shredded chicken meat to the soup before serving.*

**6 cups chicken broth (skimmed)**

**1 tablespoon oil**

**1 cup chopped white onion**

**2 bell peppers, chopped**

**2 cups chopped tomato**

**2 cups chopped green chile, page 10**

**1 tablespoon garlic purée, page 12**

**1 tablespoon oregano**

**1 tablespoon pepper**

**2 tablespoons seasoning salt, optional**

GARNISH:

**6 small corn tortillas, cut lengthwise and fried until crisp**

**2 cups shredded white cheese, such as Monterey Jack**

**2 avocados, pitted, peeled and diced**

**$^1/_2$ cup chopped green onion, green part only**

**3 tablespoons chopped cilantro, optional**

In large pot, bring broth to the boil; reduce heat to simmer. In a saucepan, heat oil and sauté onion, bell peppers, tomatoes, green chiles and garlic purée until lightly translucent. Add to simmering broth. Add oregano, pepper and seasoning salt, if using. Cover pot and simmer for 20 minutes.

To serve: In each bowl, place $^1/_3$ cup cheese. Add broth and $^1/_6$ of the diced avocado. Garnish with green onion and cilantro, if using, and float tortilla strips on top.

# Sopa de Frijoles

## Bean Soup

*Makes 6 to 8 servings*

*When my amiga and editor, Susan, remodeled her kitchen into a tile-clad cocina, she said nothing was more fitting than to christen it by making a pot of Sopa de Frijoles.*

**3 cups pinto beans**

**3 qt. hot water**

**1 white onion, chopped**

**1 tablespoon dried oregano**

**2 tablespoons garlic purée, page 12**

**3 tablespoons oil**

**1 tablespoon vinegar**

**6 to 8 fresh mint leaves, chopped**

**1 tablespoon salt, or to taste**

**$^1/_2$ to 1 lb. Mexican cheese, shredded**

Pick over beans carefully, discarding any debris, and wash beans thoroughly. In an 8-quart stock pot, place beans, water, onion, dried oregano and garlic purée and bring to the boil. Simmer beans until tender, at least 2 hours. Cool, then strain, reserving liquid. Mash beans through a coarse strainer or process for a few seconds in a blender, a batch at a time. Taste and season with salt now, not before. Stir mashed beans into the reserved liquid.

Heat oil in stock pot. Combine the bean mixture, vinegar and mint; add to the hot oil and cook, stirring, 10-15 minutes. Top each serving with shredded cheese.

# Sopa de Tomate

## Tomato Soup "Served Since 1922"

**Makes 6 to 8 servings**

*Sopa de Tomate has been served every Friday at El Charro since Monica opened the restaurant in 1922. On hot days, the soup can be turned into a refreshing, chilled gazpacho by adding chopped tomatoes, cucumbers, bell peppers and dashes of Worcestershire® and Tabasco® sauces. Or it can be frozen into ice cubes to be used in Bloody Mary cocktails. If you freeze the soup, bring it to a boil slowly before serving.*

**1 qt. water**

**2 cups beef stock (or 2 additional cups water)**

**2 tablespoons oil (optional)**

**2 tablespoons flour**

**3 cups canned tomato purée (or substitute 1$^1$/$_2$ cups water mixed with 1$^1$/$_2$ cups canned tomato paste)**

**$^1$/$_2$ cup minced white onion**

**1 teaspoon salt, or to taste**

**1 tablespoon garlic purée, page 12**

**$^3$/$_4$ cup sugar**

**12 oz. evaporated milk (or nonfat evaporated milk)**

**GARNISH:**

**4 hard-cooked eggs, chopped (optional)**

**1 cup chopped parsley**

**1 cup crumbled totopos (corn chips, page 27)**

In an 8-quart stock pot, bring water and stock to the boil.

Meanwhile, in a skillet, lightly brown flour in oil over low heat. Stir browned flour into boiling stock. After cooking mixture 10 minutes until slightly thickened, add tomato purée, onion, salt, garlic and sugar. Add evaporated milk. Set soup aside 10 minutes to allow flavors to blend. Taste and adjust seasonings.

Garnish with chopped eggs, parsley and *totopos*.

**LOW-FAT NOTITA:** *To lower the fat and calories, substitute nonfat evaporated milk or even water, and eliminate or diminish the amount of chopped-egg garnish.*

# Albóndigas

## Meatball Soup

**Makes 6 to 8 servings**

*I crave a better translation for Albóndigas. "Meatball" just doesn't seem right for this ethereal soup.*

**BROTH:**

**3 qt. water**

**1 whole white onion**

**2 ripe tomatoes, minced**

**3 green onions, chopped**

**$^1$/$_2$ cup fresh cilantro (substitute fresh parsley or 1 teaspoon dried coriander)**

**2 teaspoons dried oregano**

**MEATBALLS:**

**2 lb. ground chuck, 90% lean**

**$^1$/$_2$ cup garlic purée, page 12**

**1 egg**

**1 teaspoon salt, or to taste**

**1 teaspoon ground black pepper**

**$^1$/$_2$ cup flour (or 1 slice wet bread)**

**6 to 8 fresh mint leaves, chopped (optional)**

**$^1$/$_4$ cup uncooked rice (optional)**

In an 8-quart stock pot, bring water to the boil. Add onion. Meanwhile, in a large bowl, mix ground chuck with remaining meatball ingredients, including the rice and mint, if desired. Form mixture into balls the size of walnuts. Carefully add meatballs to boiling water, reduce heat and simmer 30 minutes, skimming off froth frequently.

**NOTITA:** *Try to use fresh mint for this one. It really makes a difference.*

About 15 minutes before soup is finished, add tomatoes, green onions, cilantro and dried oregano. Taste and adjust seasonings. Serve as a first course with 3 meatballs or as a main meal with more meatballs.

**LOW-FAT NOTITA:** *Reduce fat and calories by substituting ground turkey for beef and using egg whites or egg substitute in place of whole eggs.*

## About Albóndigas

Albóndigas is the only soup we make that does not call for stock. The simmering meatballs create their own stock. Note that if you use frozen and defrosted ground beef, the meatballs tend to turn pink.

I like to serve Albóndigas as a first course by placing 3 meatballs into a small soup bowl and ladling the broth over them. As a main course, I usually serve 6 meatballs, with a side dish of Frijoles Refritos and corn or flour tortillas. Or, for a change, serve it with French bread, which has been a welcome alternative to tortillas in the Mexican diet ever since the French influence of Emperor Maximilian in the 1860s.

# Sopa de Campanas Mixtas

## Mixed-Pepper Bisque

**Makes 6 to 8 servings**

*We like this soup served steaming hot in winter. However, in warmer months it is delightful when served chilled.*

*Campana means bell in Spanish.*

**PEPPER PURÉE:**

**6 bell peppers, red, green and gold**

**2 fresh Anaheim chiles, roasted, page 10**

**1 onion, chopped**

**2 carrots, chopped**

First, cut wafer-thin slices from each pepper to garnish soup. Set aside.

Remove and discard seeds and veins from remaining peppers, and chop.

Place chopped peppers along with chiles, onion and carrots in large kettle of boiling water and simmer until soft. Drain. Purée the vegetables in blender or food processor.

Meanwhile, combine the following in large pot:

**3 cups broth**

**1 cup water**

**1 cup milk or cream**

**1 cup chopped green onion**

**1/4 cup garlic purée, page 12**

**2 cups cubed cooked potatoes**

**1 cup cubed cooked squash**

**1/2 cup chopped fresh basil**

**1/4 teaspoon fresh ground black pepper**

Bring above to the boil. Reduce heat. Slowly add purée, stirring constantly, and allow to simmer (not boil) for 10 minutes to reduce slightly and to blend flavors. Serve in warm bowls and garnish with reserved pepper slivers.

# Sopa de Purée de Papas

## Mashed-Potato Soup

**Makes 6 to 8 servings**

*One of our favorite potato soups—other than Caldo de Queso (page 38)—is Mashed-Potato Soup with corn and chipotle chile.*

**1 onion, chopped**

**Vegetable oil spray**

**2 cups chicken stock or water**

**1 1/2 cups milk**

**3 lb. new or red potatoes, cubed**

**1 tablespoon margarine**

**1 (15 oz.) can creamed corn**

**1/4 cup garlic purée, page 12**

**Salt and pepper to taste**

**2 chipotle chiles**

**GARNISH:**

**Tortilla chips**

**Sour cream**

**Green onion, chopped**

Coat stock pot with vegetable oil spray and sauté onion quickly. Add a little water and sweat onion. Add chicken stock or water, milk, margarine and cubed potatoes. Cook uncovered until potatoes are tender. Drain and transfer to food processor or blender.

Add creamed corn and garlic purée and blend until smooth. (This can be done in batches if your processor is small.) Return to pot.

Cut chipotles into 1/4-inch dice and grind smooth with mortar and pestle—or by working a fork against the bottom and sides of a rough-textured bowl—until they form a paste. Stir into potato mixture and bring to the boil. Ladle into bowls and garnish with baked tortilla chips and dollops of sour cream mixed with chopped green onion.

**LOW-FAT NOTITA:** *A low-fat version of the potato soup uses nonfat milk and nonfat sour cream.*

# Posole

## Pork and Hominy Soup

Makes 8 to 12 servings

*In the Southwest we can find bags of prepared hominy at the meat counter. The white corn has swollen nearly triple in size after being processed in dolomitic lime (slaked lime) and water. Canned whole hominy will work, too, but rinse it well before adding to this rich soup. In the authentic recipes from Jalisco, oxtails and pigs' heads are the prized ingredients. Our family has settled for cubed, boneless pork.*

*Make posole vegetarian by omitting the pork.*

1 lb. whole hominy, rinsed well

5 cups cold water

2 lb. boneless pork, cut into 4 pieces

3 cups cold water

2 tablespoons oil

2 medium onions, chopped

2 whole heads garlic, partially separated

1 tablespoon crushed oregano

1 tablespoon salt or to taste

4 cups cooked pinto beans, page 49

2 cups strained beef broth or reserved pork broth

2 whole dried red chiles, seeded, chopped

2 whole fresh Anaheim chiles, chopped

GARNISH:

Chopped tomatoes, oregano, salsa

In covered stock pot, simmer hominy in 5 cups water for 4 hours, until kernels burst open ("flower") and are tender. Add hot water as necessary.

In another pot, simmer pork in 3 cups water with garlic about 30 minutes, until tender. Cool and drain, reserving broth. Cut meat into ³/₄-inch cubes and set aside.

While meat is cooling, heat vegetable oil in large skillet. Lightly brown onions in oil.

Add cubed pork and oregano to hominy mixture and simmer 2 more hours. Taste and season with salt.

Add cooked pinto beans to broth, stir and adjust seasoning. Add chiles and stir gently.

Serve in large soup bowls, garnish with chopped tomatoes, oregano and salsa.

# Cocido

## Vegetable and Beef Soup

Makes 12 servings

*Cocido is such a simple name for a simple soup that can be embellished into a colorful masterpiece . . . and eaten partly with your hands! Usually the soup is served in a wide, shallow soup plate. Each serving traditionally contains a 2-inch piece of corn on the cob, a beef short rib or two and totopitos (corn tortilla strips) as garnish.*

*Traditionally you eat the corn as you would corn on the cob; likewise the short ribs. A few warmed tortillas and pieces of cheese are served with the soup. A perfect dessert is fruit and cookies.*

4 qt. water

1 tablespoon vegetable oil

2 lb. beef short ribs with bone

2 carrots, chopped

1 onion, sliced

1 teaspoon salt

1 teaspoon pepper

To complete:

CHOOSE FROM THESE SUGGESTED VEGETABLES:

Potatoes, carrots, onions, celery, whole string beans, zucchini or other squash, lima beans, peas, garbanzo beans (canned), corn niblets (canned), chopped tomatoes, corn on the cob

SEASON TO TASTE WITH:

Salt and pepper, oregano, basil, parsley or cilantro

GARNISH:

Salsa, tortilla strips, shredded or crumbled cheese

Bring water to the boil in large stock pot.

Meanwhile, in large skillet, brown short ribs in lightly oiled skillet. Add carrots and onions and brown slightly.

Add browned ingredients to hot water (or stock) and simmer, covered 45 minutes. Skim froth frequently.

LOW-FAT NOTITA: *At this point, the soup can be held, chilled, defatted and refrigerated until ready to complete.*

Cut more vegetables of your choice into bite-size pieces and add to simmering stock and short ribs, adding the quickest-cooking vegetables last. Season to taste with salt, pepper and herbs.

To serve: With tongs, remove a piece of corn on the cob and a short rib or two and place in soup plate. Ladle broth and vegetables over the corn and meat. Top with a sprinkling of fried corn tortilla strips (*Totopitos*). Pass salsa and cheese.

NOTITA: *If you have beef broth saved from preparing shredded beef, Machaca (page 72), use that in this recipe rather than starting from scratch.*

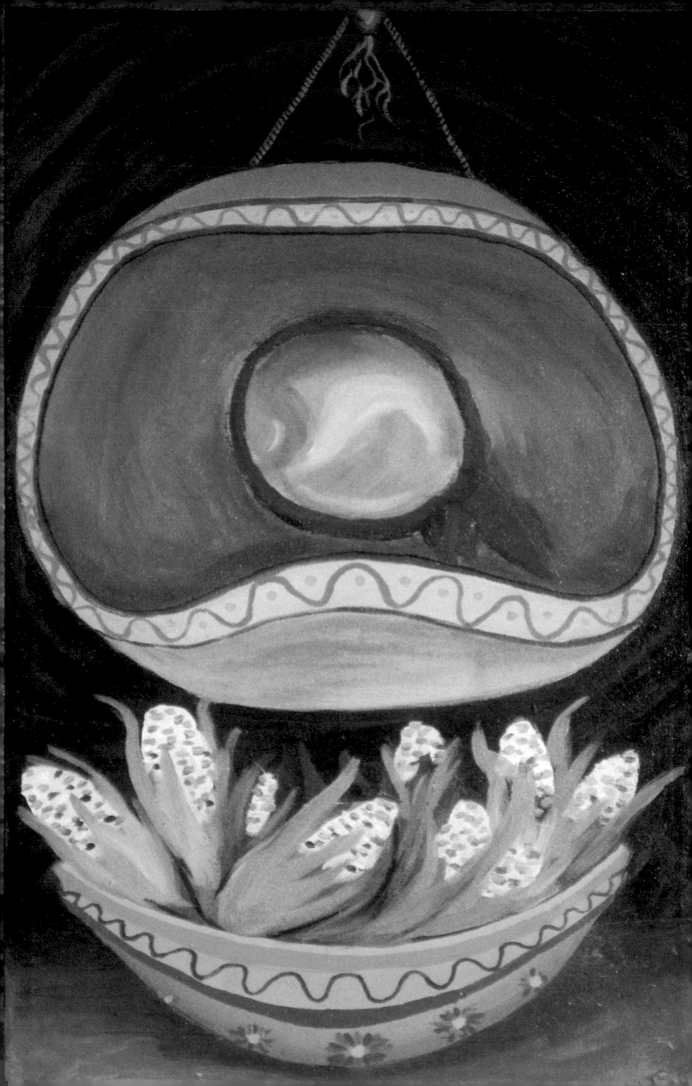

# Rice, Pasta, Beans and Vegetables

## Arroz, Pasta, Frijoles y Verduras

*For rice in the Americas, we thank the Chinese; for pasta, too, through the Italians. But for most of our vegetables, we thank the New World. Corn, squash, chiles and beans, potatoes, tomatoes, onions and garlic were all here for the picking when the Europeans arrived.*

**Photo on page 44-45: left to right—Frijoles de la Olla with Fresh Tomato Condiment, Arroz Estilo El Charro**

In addition to rice and exotic vegetables, the Chinese influence in Mexico and Tucson shows up in arts and crafts. Paper—in particular, thin, colorful tissue paper—was brought to Mexico by Chinese merchants who did business along Mexico's Pacific coast. Perhaps the fine but cheap paper was used to wrap precious fruits and vegetables or pieces of porcelain for transport across the Pacific. Whatever, the Mexicans were intrigued by its colors and its adaptability. On fiesta days, citizens decorated their homes, plazas and streets with rectangles of red, green, yellow and blue sheets of Chinese tissue paper strung on lines, creating garlands or banners. The papers were cut like coarse lace, enabling wind and sunlight to make a celebration even more joyous. These were called **banderas de papel picado**. Today, as you travel through Mexican villages and big cities alike, you will see remnants of banderas, perhaps faded, fluttering in the wind along fences or from telephone poles, left over from the most recent fiesta.

**Piñatas**, colorful, candy-filled toys seen at children's parties, were once made around clay pots and layered with strips of **papel picado** (cut paper). Plain pots, or pots shaped like burros, pigs, even human-like figures, were covered with shreds of colored tissue paper attached with homemade glue made of cornstarch and water. These were filled with fruit, nuts and candy. A blindfolded child would be given a stick or bat. The piñata was usually suspended by rope over the limb of a tree. The end not attached to the piñata would be held by an older child or adult who could lift and lower the piñata at will, making the game easy or difficult for the contender. He or she would wave the stick in the air, hoping to make robust contact with the fragile pot, breaking it and scattering the contents onto the ground for friends to scramble after.

Today, piñatas are formed on a base of harmless papier-mâché. The adaptability of papier-mâché has encouraged even more diverse piñata shapes. It is not unusual to see cartoon characters, Santa Claus, extraterrestrials and political figures made into plump piñatas.

**Cascarones** are party favors, similar in spirit to British crackers or noisemakers. Blown egg shells filled with confetti are perched on top of long, skinny paper cones, studded with colorful sand (originally) or glitter from the craft store (these days), then adorned with streamers made of colored tissue paper. Cascarones are traditionally cracked over someone's head.

To make **papel picado**, fold tissue-paper sheets several times before cutting—as you did to make paper snowflakes in first grade. Some people turn the simple craft into an art, creating ingeniously thought-out patterns that represent scenes. Others present the papel picado folded, so that when opened, a story of intricate detail unfolds with it.

Lately I have noticed banderas made from sheets of plastic, presumably so they will last from one fiesta to the next. To me they are just not the same—just as plastic, electrified luminarias we see around Tucson at Christmas are missing the unique glow the original paper sacks provided.

# Rice, Pasta and Dry Soup

In Mexican culture, we thrive on *sopa seca*, which literally means "dry soup" and figuratively, a very thick soup or stew. Usually sopas secas are based on rice or pasta. Before these were available, they were likely to be made with corn mush or tortillas. Spanish paella is a good example of a modern sopa seca. Some of our favorites are *Arroz con Plátanos* (Rice with Bananas), opposite page, and *Sopa Seca de Fideo* (Vermicelli Soup), page 49.

I think the early Asian influence in Mexican households has a lot to do with Mexicans' passion for white rice. However, why we call rice steamed with vegetables "Spanish rice" I cannot explain. Others call it *Sopa de Arroz*—yet another *sopa seca*—but either way I love it and I love it in particular with hot yellow mustard.

# Arroz Estilo El Charro

*El Charro Rice with Tomato*

### Makes 6 to 8 servings

*When served as a side dish, rice is usually fixed this way, with a few token vegetables for color. As a main dish, a sopa seca, it is much heartier, with pieces of potato, meat, poultry or shrimp.*

The trick is to cook the rice in a dry pan until it pops. *It actually begins to explode, like popcorn. This seems to help the rice absorb the flavors of added ingredients and to develop a soft but distinct texture.*

**2 tablespoons oil**

**1 small onion, chopped**

**2 cups uncooked long-grain rice**

**1 teaspoon salt, or to taste**

**4 cups stock or half water**

**1 tablespoon ground hot red chile, optional**

**$^1/_2$ cup tomato sauce**

**$^1/_2$ cup garlic purée, or to taste, page 12**

**1 cup frozen peas and carrots**

**1 tomato, chopped**

Heat oil in a large skillet. Lightly brown chopped onion. Add rice and stir constantly over low heat until rice starts to brown. (Be careful not to let it get too brown.) Add salt and stock. Add ground red chile, if using. Increase heat and bring to the boil; reduce heat, cover tightly and simmer 10 minutes. Add tomato sauce, garlic purée, peas, carrots and chopped tomato and stir. Cover and cook about 20 minutes, until rice is tender. Uncover during the last few minutes of cooking if you want the rice to be on the dry side. Let rice sit 15 minutes, then fluff with two forks.

**Variation:** Add cooked chicken or shrimp or both for a hearty main dish.

**NOTITA:** *A piece of foil under the cover will help create a tight fit so the rice steams to perfection.*

# Arroz con Fruta

*Rice Flavored with Fruit*

### Makes 6 servings

*The sweetness of the fruit in the rice is especially appealing when served with a picante-sauced meat, such as Pork Tenderloin with Mango (page 84.)*

**2 cups long-grain white rice**

**4 cups water**

**$^1/_2$ teaspoon salt**

**CHOOSE FROM:**

**Dried cranberries, raisins, chopped prunes, apricots, pineapple, orange or tangerine segments**

Wash rice in cold water. Drain. Place in heavy 2-quart saucepan. Add water. Cover, bring to the boil. Quickly stir in $^1/_4$ cup to 1 cup fruit of your choice. Cover immediately and reduce heat to lowest setting; cook until rice is tender and water is absorbed. Let sit covered off heat for several minutes. Fluff with fork before serving.

**NOTITA:** *Leftover rice becomes a healthful snack when topped with plain yogurt.*

# Arroz con Plátanos

*White Rice with Bananas*

### Makes 8 servings

*My dad loved to eat white rice with fried bananas, a dish his family's Chinese cook prepared. He probably had this popular dish in Mexico, too, with plantains (a type of banana), which are very starchy, hard and bitter. Plantains must be cooked; they are never eaten raw like our bananas. Today local supermarkets readily carry this fruit, which you will recognize as being small and almost black. I still prefer to use regular bananas that are firm and green-skinned.*

*A touch of hot mustard adds a spark to this recipe.*

**$^1/_3$ cup oil**

**2 firm green bananas (or plantains)**

**3 cups cooked white rice**

Heat oil in deep skillet. Peel and slice bananas or plantains diagonally into $^1/_2$-inch pieces. Fry in hot oil, turning once, until light brown. Serve atop bowls of hot rice.

**NOTITA:** *I recently used this rice dish as stuffing for a chimichanga and it was a big hit.*

# Pasta

Some of the best Italian restaurants anywhere are in Mexico City. Mexicans are not strangers to pasta.

The most popular pasta in Mexican cuisine is *fideo*, similar to vermicelli—fine, long noodles used in soups and as side dishes. Macaroni, shells, lasagna, fettuccine, spaghetti and ravioli are often used in Mexican dishes. However, it is fideo that I feel fits most authentically in our cooking, as in our *Sopa Seca de Fideo* (opposite).

Sopa seca or "dry soup" isn't exactly the perfect name. (Neither is "refried beans" for *frijoles refritos,* which are fried once, not twice.) Sopas secas are hardly dry. Perhaps "pasta stew" would be more descriptive. Nonetheless, sopa seca is what it is and always has been.

We serve *Sopa Seca de Fideo* as a light dish by itself, or more often as a side dish. At home, leftover meat and vegetables find a second life in the next day's sopas secas.

# Beans

Mexico is—and has been for 500 years, probably longer—as much a melting pot as the United States has been for 300 years. Monica's melting-pot style of cooking—or as much of it as I can preserve—prevails at El Charro, so you will find garbanzo beans (chickpeas) tossed in with the vegetable garnish, just as a reminder of the riches out there.

There is nothing complicated about making a great pot of beans, just some rules.

★ Never add cold water to beans that are cooking; only boiling water. Cold water darkens beans.

★ Do not add salt until beans are at least half-cooked, otherwise the beans will be tough. And remember, as liquid reduces, the salty taste intensifies. So, undersalt to begin with, and adjust to taste when beans are ready to serve.

★ It is not necessary to presoak beans before cooking.

## Cool Water

An *olla* is a cooking vessel, traditionally fat and round with a flat bottom, made of clay.

Before homes in the desert had plumbing and refrigerators, a family would fill a large *olla* with drinking water and hang it in the shade where the water would cool considerably on summer days. The porous clay would allow some evaporation and thus, through a law of physics intuitively understood by the ancients, the water inside would lose heat.

# Sopa Seca de Fideo

## Vermicelli "Soup"

**Makes 6 to 8 servings**

*Think of the variations this catch-all recipe could have, from macaroni and cheese to any number of casseroles based on a variety of pasta— hot or cold!*

**2 lb. coiled fideos (vermicelli)**

**$^1/_4$ cup oil**

**1 cup tomato sauce**

**1 teaspoon salt, or to taste**

**$^1/_4$ cup garlic purée, page 12**

**1 white onion, chopped**

**6 cups hot chicken or beef stock, page 35**

**$^1/_2$ cup chopped bell pepper**

**1 cup chopped fresh tomato**

**1 cup shredded longhorn cheese, or other cheese**

**GARNISH:**

**1 cup shredded additional cheese**

Heat oil in a skillet, and lightly brown fideos coils on both sides. Transfer to a 4-quart saucepan. Add remaining ingredients, except cheese, and simmer over low heat 20 minutes. Stir once or twice, separating coils with a long fork. Continue cooking, uncovered, until all the liquid has been absorbed. Add cheese and stir. Garnish with additional cheese.

# Frijoles de la Olla

## Whole Beans

**Makes 6 to 8 servings**

*One of our favorite ways to eat Frijoles de la Olla is with a fresh-tomato condiment. I've included that recipe at right.*

**2 cups pinto beans**

**2 qt. water**

**1 whole head garlic, peeled and mashed**

**Salt to taste**

Pick over beans carefully, discarding any debris, and rinse the beans thoroughly. Place in an 8-quart stock pot with 2 quarts cold water. Add garlic and bring to the boil. Immediately reduce heat and cook slowly, undisturbed, until beans are very tender, at least 2 hours. Salt lightly.

**NOTITA:** *Stirring beans clouds the broth. This is not bad, but it is not the sign of a confident cocinera.*

**Variation:** You will often find beans cooked with ham hocks or bacon, onion and spiced with oregano or, in Texas, cumin. Sometimes it's hard to leave them simple!

**NOTITA:** *Beans sour if covered and refrigerated while they are still hot. If you make a big batch, cool them before storing by spreading them in a roasting pan, preferably one that will nestle inside a larger roasting pan filled with cold water, which speeds the cooling.*

# Fresh-Tomato Condiment

**2 fresh tomatoes, chopped**

**1 tablespoon fresh oregano**

**Sprinkle of white vinegar**

**Dab of sour cream, optional**

**1 onion, chopped**

Mix all ingredients.

# El Charro Frijoles Refritos

## Refried Beans

**Makes 6 to 8 servings**

*The traditional—and tastiest— method of preparing Frijoles Refritos calls for lard or bacon fat, evaporated milk and lots of cheese. Lard is 99% of the reason beans taste so good. If you want heart-healthier refried beans, use canola oil instead of the lard or bacon fat.*

**4 cups cooked pinto beans, recipe this page**

**2 tablespoons melted lard, hot bacon fat or canola oil**

**1 (12 oz.) can evaporated milk**

**$^1/_2$ lb. longhorn cheese or Mexican cheese, shredded**

**Salsa de Chile Colorado, page 63**

**Additional lard, bacon fat or oil**

Mash cooked beans in skillet and add hot lard or bacon fat. Mix well. Stir in evaporated milk. Cook over very low heat, stirring frequently.

**Variation:** Beans can be served at this point, without the cheese, salsa or additional fat. Or these can be added and the beans truly "refried" in a bit more smoking-hot fat just before serving.

# Vegetables

Over the years we have added more vegetables to our recipe collection. Vegetables lend a healthy goodness to dishes, along with taste, color and texture. The recipes are endless, from our black-bean-and-corn salad, full of fresh fragrant herbs and crunchy peppers, to a filling of spinach and tomato for our stuffed quesadillas. Only the seasons dictate the abundant resources of fresh natural ingredients.

For fall, rich-tasting, glorious squashes make some of our best *sopas.* In winter, the delicious variety of chiles grace some of our best meat dishes. For spring, light and colorful greens make up some of our customers' favorite seasonal salads. In summer, what better way to cool down than with a delicious salsa made from fresh root vegetables, a squeeze of lime, and a sprinkling of chopped chiles. Vegetables make every part of the meal interesting and add pizzazz to almost everyone's palate.

# Lent and Meatless Meals

At El Charro, we continue to observe Lent by preparing several dishes that we do not offer during the rest of the year. Many of our foods are tied to the church calendar—red tamales for Christmas or *Quelites con Frijoles* for Lent.

During Lent, when meatless meals mean extra care and concern for balanced nutrition, we look to vegetables to meet our needs. At other times of the year, when we want something special to accompany a chop or burger or chicken breast, we look again to our Lenten vegetables. Spinach (*quelite*) is one of these vegetables.

We use quelite, sometimes called *espinaca,* raw or slightly wilted, with a hot dressing or other warm topping, or cooked through and tossed with hot *fideo* or *frijoles enteros* (whole beans, page 49). Sometimes we add it, roughly chopped, to rice and vegetable soups.

The dish we serve at El Charro on Fridays during Lent, along with the cod entrée (*Pescado Viscayena,* page 96), is called simply *Quelites.* We toss whole cooked pinto beans (cooked without smoked pork—just salt, pepper, onion and garlic) with fresh, steamed spinach. It's a satisfying marriage of flavors and textures. To round out the plate, we serve an Enchilada Sonorense (page 27), El Charro Rice (page 47) and Capirotada (page 115) for dessert.

# Torta de Desayuno
## Mexican Brunch Pie

### Makes 6 to 8 servings

Egg pies are easy to make. I created one out of odds and ends in the pantry and it turned out so well I added it to my repertoire.

**Pastry for 1-crust pie (See page 82, Empanada Pastry)**

FILLING:

**$^1/_4$ cup flour**

**$^1/_2$ teaspoon salt**

**$^1/_2$ teaspoon ground white pepper**

**$^1/_2$ teaspoon red pepper flakes**

**$^1/_2$ cup crumbled Mexican cheese (or cheese of preference)**

**6 eggs beaten**

**1 cup hot milk**

**2 tablespoons chopped green onion**

**6 fresh Anaheim chiles, roasted, page 10, chopped**

**1 cup canned kernel corn**

Line a large pie plate with pastry, giving it a generous lip to accommodate the puffing of the egg mixture during baking.

Preheat oven to 325°F (165°C). In a large bowl, mix together the dry ingredients and cheese. Add the beaten eggs and hot milk and mix thoroughly. Fold in onion, chile and corn. Pour mixture in prepared pie plate. Bake 30 to 40 minutes or until filling is set. (A knife inserted in the center of the pie should come out clean.)

**NOTITA:** *Nonvegetarian egg pies are easily made. Experiment with adding browned chorizo, sautéed sliced mushrooms or cooked bacon, different varieties of cheese and cooked vegetables. Most of the meat, chicken and fish fillings described in this book can be added. This is an especially good place to use leftovers.*

*Egg substitute works beautifully if you want a less-rich product.*

# Quelites con Frijoles
## Spinach and Beans

### Makes 6 to 8 servings

This spinach dish may be used as a filling for enchiladas or chalupas. It is served with the Lenten meal at El Charro.

**4 bunches fresh spinach, or 2 (10 oz.) pkg. frozen chopped spinach**

**1 tablespoon oil**

**$^1/_2$ cup minced white onion**

**1 tablespoon garlic purée, page 12**

**$^1/_2$ cup crumbled Mexican cheese**

**$^1/_2$ cup half-and-half**

**1 cup Frijoles de la Olla (whole cooked pinto beans, page 49)**

Rinse fresh spinach and steam 10 minutes in small amount of water. Drain and chop. Or thaw, cook and drain frozen spinach.

In a large skillet, sauté onions in oil until translucent. Add garlic purée. Stir in spinach and cheese. Stir in half-and-half and boil 3 minutes. Add beans and simmer a few minutes.

**Variation: Spinach and Nuts for Enchiladas**

Eliminate the pinto beans in *Quelites con Frijoles* and add about $^1/_2$ cup chopped walnuts or pecans. Place filling on softened corn tortillas, roll and place seam side down in a baking dish. Top with *Salsa de Chile Colorado* (page 63) and cheese. Bake at 325°F (165°C) until cheese bubbles. Serve with rice flavored with chicken- or vegetable stock and refried beans.

**NOTITA:** *Add a little crumbled cheese and a bit of salsa to the Quelites con Frijoles, wrap it all in a tortilla, and you have a lovely spinach burro. Sometimes we use quelites blended with nuts and cheese as filling for enchiladas.*

# Papas y Chiles
## Fried Potatoes and Chiles for Taco Filling

### Makes 4 to 6 servings

**1 lb. new potatoes**

**1 onion sliced**

**2 fresh Anaheim chiles, roasted, page 10, diced**

**Oil for sautéing**

**Salt and pepper to taste**

Cut and boil potatoes until cooked but firm. Peel if desired. When cool enough to handle, slice coarsely and drain on paper toweling.

In large skillet, heat 1 tablespoon oil. Sauté sliced onion until soft; if needed, add more oil and add potatoes, shaking pan to distribute oil. Cook over medium heat, shaking pan often until potatoes are lightly browned. Stir in diced chiles. Season with salt and pepper. Use as filling for tacos.

# Rajas con Crema y Piñones

## Creamed Green Chile with Pine Nuts

Makes 6 to 8 servings

*Rajas are thin strips of something, in this case green chiles. They are stewed with cream and served as a vegetable side dish. The chile, onion and garlic mixture can be prepared ahead and heated with cream, cheese and pine nuts just before serving.*

**1 onion sliced**

**$^1/_4$ cup garlic purée, page 12**

**12 fresh Anaheim chiles, roasted, page 10, thinly sliced**

**$^1/_2$ teaspoon salt (omit if using feta cheese)**

**1 cup cream, sour cream or nonfat sour cream**

**$^1/_2$ cup crumbled Mexican or feta cheese**

**1 teaspoon dried oregano**

**1 tablespoon toasted piñones (optional)**

Sauté onion with garlic in a nonstick skillet. Add chile strips and salt, and sauté until warmed through. Add cream or nonfat sour cream a little at a time, stirring carefully until thick enough to cover chiles. Add oregano and crumbled cheese; stir.

To serve: Sprinkle with piñones that have been toasted briefly in a dry skillet, if desired.

**NOTITA:** *Monica probably used homemade crème fraîche in these dishes. A facsimile of the rich French crème fraîche can be made by mixing heavy cream and nonfat sour cream. It is lighter in fat and calories and holds up well on steamed fresh spinach or carrots or other cooked vegetables.*

*Mexican fresh cream is available in some southwestern supermarkets.*

# Ejotes con Crema y Almendras

## String Beans with Cream and Almonds

Makes 6 to 8 servings

*This recipe is similar to Rajas con Crema y Piñones. The basic idea is adaptable to other vegetables and combinations: zucchini and red onion or chiles and yellow squash.*

**1 lb. to 1$^1/_2$ lb. fresh green beans; or 2 (16-oz.) cans French-style green beans**

**6 green onions**

**$^1/_4$ cup garlic purée, page 12**

**1 tablespoon olive oil or vegetable oil**

**$^1/_2$ teaspoon salt (omit if using feta cheese)**

**$^1/_2$ teaspoon ground white pepper**

**1 cup sour cream**

**$^1/_2$ cup crumbled Mexican or feta cheese**

**$^1/_2$ cup slivered almonds**

If using fresh green beans, snap off the ends, string them if necessary and slice lengthwise. Steam or boil until partially cooked and tender-crisp.

Mince green onion, reserving 1 tablespoon green tops for garnish.

In large skillet, heat oil and sauté onion with garlic. Add beans and salt and sauté until warmed through. Add sour cream a little at a time, stirring carefully until mixture is thick enough to coat beans. Add crumbled cheese; stir. Adjust seasoning.

To serve: Top individual servings or serving bowl with reserved minced onion tops and slivered almonds.

**LOW-FAT NOTITA:** *The low-fat variations include using nonfat sour cream, less cheese and reducing the amount of oil used to sauté.*

# Papas Molidas de Navidad

## Christmas Mashed Potatoes

*Makes 6 to 8 servings*

*On special days, such as Thanksgiving and Christmas, our family enhances mashed potatoes by adding colorful but mild green-chile flecks—like confetti—and a daub of red salsa nestled into a central well of the dish. It may remind you of the Christmas wreath. The extra flavor is especially good with roast turkey.*

**6 medium potatoes, peeled and diced**

**1 (15 oz.) can evaporated milk**

**Salt and pepper to taste**

**2 tablespoons butter or margarine**

**1 cup fresh Anaheim chile, roasted, page 10, diced**

**1 cup salsa, page 62**

Cook potatoes in water until soft. Drain and mash. Beat in evaporated milk, salt, pepper and butter and whip until potatoes are fluffy. Fold in diced chile.

To serve: With a large spoon, make an indentation in the mound of potatoes in the serving bowl. Place the salsa into the well.

**NOTITA:** *A trick we use to lower fat content in recipes calling for softened tortillas is to dip the tortillas in a Vegetable Broth (recipe follows) rather than oil. This broth is also the underlying sauce base for several vegetarian fillings for enchiladas.*

# Caldo de Verduras

## Vegetable Broth

To make the broth, cook equal amounts of minced onion, tomatoes and green chiles in a small amount of water until they are soft. Add minced garlic, salt and pepper, oregano, cilantro and other seasonings to taste. Add more water to cover ingredients and simmer, covered, over low heat for 20 minutes, adding water if necessary. Cool and refrigerate, covered.

# Ejotes con Chile Colorado

## String Beans with Red Chile Sauce

*Makes 6 to 8 servings*

*Green beans are elevated to new "high" when given the red-chile treatment. Garnish with slivered almonds if you like.*

**1/2 cup vegetable oil**

**1/4 cup garlic purée, page 12**

**2 cups Salsa de Chile Colorado, page 63**

**Salt and pepper to taste**

**1 lb. fresh or frozen green beans, cut and cooked**

Heat oil, garlic purée and Salsa de Chile Colorado in a large skillet. Cook over very low heat for 15 minutes, stirring frequently to prevent scorching. Add cooked beans and heat through.

**NOTITA:** *To make as a main dish, heat 2 cups cooked and cubed chicken with beans and top with shredded cheese. We enjoy this spicy green-bean dish with a plate of warm flour tortillas, or wrapped in tortillas, burro-style.*

# Enchiladas de Hongos

## Mushroom Enchiladas

*Makes 4 servings*

**1 lb. mushrooms, cubed (or left whole if small)**

**1 cup cooked cubed carrots**

**1/2 cup cooked peas**

**1 cup cooked cubed potato**

**1 cup diced fresh Anaheim chile, roasted, page 10**

**1 cup sour cream or plain yogurt**

**1 cup diced avocado, optional**

**Seasoning: cilantro, parsley, oregano, salt and pepper**

**2 cups Vegetable Broth, opposite**

**8 corn tortillas**

**Shredded longhorn cheese or other cheese**

Sauté mushrooms, carrots, peas and chile approximately 10 minutes in a pan prepared with vegetable spray. Remove from pan and combine vegetables with sour cream and seasonings. (You may refrigerate the filling at this point for later use.)

Preheat oven to 350°F (175°C). In a shallow saucepan, heat broth to simmer. Dip each corn tortilla in broth, place on heat-proof platter. Place 1 to 2 tablespoons mushroom-vegetable filling on tortilla; roll and place seam side down in a baking dish. Repeat with remaining tortillas. Spoon remaining filling over enchiladas. Cover with cheese and bake until cheese bubbles.

**NOTITA:** *For mushroom fillings, we add the whole or cut-up mushrooms to the sauté during the last few minutes of cooking so they do not become overcooked.*

*Photo on pages 54-55: left to right—Calabacitas con Queso, Papas Molidas de Navidad, Ejotes con Chile Colorado, Chile Relleno*

# Calabacitas con Queso

*Squash with Cheese*

### Makes 6 to 8 servings

*For Calabacitas con Queso, I like to use zucchini, small patty-pan or yellow crookneck squash, either separately or in combination. Storage makes squash bitter, so cook it soon after purchase or harvest.*

*There are almost no rules for this one, except to add the cheese just before serving. For a festive look, garnish with red bell pepper strips.*

**2 tablespoons oil**

**1 white onion, chopped**

**10 medium squash, cut into 1-inch chunks**

**3 tomatoes, chopped**

**$^1/_4$ cup garlic purée, page 12**

**$^1/_4$ cup water**

**2 fresh Anaheim chiles, roasted, page 10, chopped**

**8 oz. can kernel corn, drained**

**$^1/_2$ lb. longhorn cheese, shredded**

In a large skillet, heat oil and sauté onion, squash, tomatoes and garlic purée. Add water, cover and cook over low heat 20 minutes. When squash is tender, add chopped chiles and corn, and stir lightly. Taste, and season with salt and pepper. Cook 5 minutes more. Turn off heat. Immediately sprinkle with cheese, then cover for a few minutes so cheese melts.

**NOTITA:** *Calabacitas can be prepared and refrigerated ahead of serving, up to the point of adding the cheese. When ready to serve, warm squash mixture slowly over low heat, then stir in cheese, cover and set aside 5 minutes.*

**Variation:** If you have any leftover *Calabacitas*, purée it, then blend with 3 cups beef stock, a little milk and seasonings to your taste, and you will have *Sopa de Calabacitas*.

For a vegetarian Calabacitas soup, use milk (1% or canned low fat) instead of beef stock.

# Calabaza Dulce

*Sweet Banana Squash*

### Makes 6 to 8 servings

*We serve sweetened squash as a side dish, warm or cold. It complements particularly spicy dishes. At times we serve Calabaza Dulce for dessert, garnished with whipped cream and chopped nuts.*

**3 lb. banana squash**

**1 cup brown sugar or 1 cone piloncillo**

**$^3/_4$ cup water**

**GARNISH:**

**1 cup heavy cream, whipped (sweetened if desired)**

**$1^1/_4$ cups chopped nuts**

Clean and peel squash and remove seeds. Cut into 2-inch cubes. In a 4-quart saucepan, bring water, squash and brown sugar to the boil. Lower heat, cover and simmer 15 to 20 minutes. Uncover and cook 15 minutes more or until squash is tender.

Mash; adjust seasonings. Serve warm or chilled, topped with whipped cream and nuts.

# Rajitas de Nopalitos y Cebollitas

*Sautéed Prickly Pear with Onions and Green Chiles*

### Makes approximately 2 cups

*Prepare nopales according to the directions on page 11.*

**1 tablespoon vegetable oil**

**12 prepared nopales, page 11, cut into strips**

**6 fresh Anaheim chiles, roasted, page 10, cut into strips**

**1 white onion, sliced**

**$^1/_2$ cup beer or water**

**8 oz. longhorn or other cheese, shredded**

In large skillet, heat oil and sauté strips of nopales, chiles and onion slices until tender. Drain oil. Add beer and bring to the boil. Fold in cheese; cover pan so cheese will melt.

**NOTITA:** *Serve with warm flour tortillas.*

**NOTITA:** *If using bottled nopalitos, be sure to rinse them before using.*

# Chiles Rellenos
## Stuffed Chiles

Makes 4 or 8 servings

*Use Anaheim chiles for this dish. Another favorite is the slightly fatter and darker—and maybe a little higher on the heat scale—pasilla or ancho chile. (See Chiles, page 9.)*

**8 fresh Anaheim chiles, roasted, page 10 (stems intact, if possible)**

**1 lb. Mexican or longhorn cheese, cut in strips**

**BATTER:**

**3 eggs**

**3 tablespoons flour**

**1 teaspoon salt**

**1 teaspoon ground black pepper**

**$^1/_4$ cup oil**

**GARNISH:**

**4 cups Taco Sauce, page 64, warmed**

**2 cups shredded longhorn cheese**

Make a 2-inch slit in chiles and insert a strip of cheese. Set aside.

Separate eggs and beat whites until stiff. Separately beat yolks and fold into whites, along with flour, salt and pepper. Meanwhile, heat oil in a large skillet. Dip stuffed chiles, one at a time, into egg batter to coat, then remove with a large spoon. Carefully lower coated chiles into hot oil, 3 or 4 at a time. Fry until golden brown on both sides.

**NoTITA:** *The chiles may be made ahead to this point and reheated in a 400°F (205°C) oven about 10 minutes before adding topping.*

To serve: Arrange on platter or individual plates and pour warm Taco Sauce over each chile. Garnish with more cheese and place under broiler to melt cheese, if desired.

**NoTITA:** *Chicken, chorizo or tuna may be used to stuff the chiles, but cheese is always a garnish.*

# Relleno de Jalapeño
## Savory Jalapeño Stuffing

Makes 12 cups, or enough for a 12- to 14-pound turkey or pork loin

*Often stuffings are misnamed. They aren't stuffed into anything but a casserole and are served as a side dish. This rich, spicy stuffing may be stuffed into a rolled pork roast or beef flank steak, a turkey or chicken—or used to fill pockets cut into thick pork chops. By itself, it is a good meatless dish.*

**$^1/_4$ lb. margarine**

**1 cup chopped onion**

**$^1/_2$ cup chopped celery**

**3 loaves commercial jalapeño-cheese bread, sliced**

**2 cups warm water**

**$^1/_2$ lb. crumbled tomato-and-basil feta cheese**

**GARNISH (optional):**

**Strips of roasted red bell pepper**

**Jalapeño slices**

Preheat oven to 400°F (205°C). In large skillet, melt margarine. Sauté onion and celery, stirring frequently.

Meanwhile lightly toast slices of jalapeño bread on cookie sheet in oven. Cut into cubes. Combine cubed jalapeño bread and water in large bowl. Fold in crumbled feta cheese.

Slowly add moistened bread to celery-and-onion mixture in skillet, stirring constantly over low heat about 5 minutes to blend flavors. Add additional margarine, if needed. Stir again. Turn into a casserole dish and garnish the top with roasted peppers and jalapeño slices, if desired.

Cover and bake at 325°F (165°C) for 20 minutes. Uncover and continue baking until browned, about another 15 minutes.

**Variation:** Crumbled, cooked chorizo adds another spicy touch to this recipe. Mix 1$^1/_2$ cups of cooked and crumbled chorizo into stuffing before turning mixture into cassarole.

**NoTITA:** *Jars of preserved roasted red bell peppers are available in the Italian-foods section in supermarkets.*

*Flavored cheese and commercial jalapeño-cheese bread make this a quickly prepared side dish.*

# Sauces

## *Salsas*

*Sauces, or salsas, are either cooked or raw (cruda) in Mexican cuisine. "Salsa" refers not only to the bright red or green condiment you find on the table next to a basket of chips, but to more refined cooking sauces as well.*

*Cooked salsas are more subtle than the brilliant fresh sauces. Served warm or chilled, they keep better than the fresh sauces.*

*The red chile we use for red chile sauce is the Anaheim or long green chile that has ripened and then dried. It is the custom to tie red chiles in elongated bunches called sartas or ristras to take to market. In Tucson, the market often turns out to be a farmer's pickup truck parked on a vacant lot near an intersection on the city's outskirts. Sometimes sartas are used as a front-door decoration or a kitchen decoration.*

*To prepare the basic red chile sauce, dried peppers are softened in boiling water, then ground into a rich red paste. The paste is thinned with cooking liquid for use as a sauce for enchiladas and other dishes. Left thick and spiced with orégano and vinegar, it becomes Salsa Adobada and is used as a marinade for carne (beef) adobada or puerco (pork) adobado (page 84).*

*Photo on page 60-61: left to right—Salsa de Chile Colorado, Escabeche, Salsa Verde para Enchiladas, Salsa de Chile Verde, Salsa para Tacos*

# Salsa de Tomatillo Cruda

## Uncooked Tomatillo and Tomato Sauce with Olives

### Makes 2 cups

Tomatillos are not tomatoes, but a member of the gooseberry family. They are smaller than a golf ball, wrapped in a papery husk. They are salty and firmer than tomatoes and usually are cooked before eating. However, I like to make a salsa cruda with raw tomatillos.

2 fresh tomatillos, chopped

2 red tomatoes, chopped

2 onions chopped

12 green olives, pitted

2 cups cherry tomatoes

$^1/_2$ cup chopped fresh basil or cilantro

Salt and pepper to taste

1 to 2 tablespoons olive oil, if desired

GARNISH:

Cilantro leaves

Combine all the ingredients in a glass bowl. Serve at once or chilled.

NOTITA: *Try this at room temperature as a vegetable along with poached salmon. It makes a heart-healthy low-fat dinner, especially if you omit the olives and use a tiny bit of oil.*

# Salsa de Chile Verde

## Chunky Green Chile and Tomato Sauce

### Makes 2 cups

At the restaurant we make several different salsas. This one is especially attractive as well as delicious.

2 cloves garlic, peeled

$^1/_2$ teaspoon salt

1 teaspoon vinegar

1 teaspoon oil

6 fresh Anaheim chiles, roasted, page 10, chopped

6 ripe tomatoes, chopped

1 medium white onion, chopped

$^1/_2$ teaspoon additional salt, or to taste

1 teaspoon ground black pepper

Chopped cilantro (optional)

Mash garlic in a small wooden salad bowl, using salt as grinding agent. Stir in vinegar and oil. Combine with remaining ingredients in larger glass bowl. Cover and chill for several hours before serving.

♥♥♥♥♥♥♥♥♥♥♥♥♥♥♥♥♥

Monica's fresh green chile salsa was a work of art. The fresh green chiles were charred before peeling, giving them a woodsy aroma and a slightly softened texture. They were chopped and combined with fresh tomatoes, garlic and onion, a little vinegar and oil, pepper and salt.

♥♥♥♥♥♥♥♥♥♥♥♥♥♥♥♥♥

# Escabeche

## Vegetable Pickle

### Makes 3 cups; 4 to 6 servings

A pickle or relish is nice to have on hand when you want to spark up what might be considered a bland meal. This escabeche is vinegary and hot. Use your favorite vegetables to marinate in the sauce—it's up to you.

$^1/_2$ cup lemon or lime juice

2 tablespoons canola oil

1 teaspoon garlic purée, page 12

1 chipotle chile, minced

2 tablespoons rice or white wine vinegar

1 bay leaf

$^1/_2$ tablespoon cayenne pepper

2 large carrots, cut into eight sticks

$^1/_2$ white onion, cut into rings

1 medium jícama, peeled and cut into sticks

Choose a variety of other vegetables: cauliflower, turnip, cucumber, zucchini or other squash, garbanzo beans, kidney beans, string beans, etc.

To make marinade: Combine juice, oil, garlic purée, chile, vinegar and spices in a jar with tight-fitting lid. Shake well.

Place cut vegetables in a nonreactive bowl, such as glass or stainless steel, and pour marinade over them. Toss to coat. Cover with plastic wrap and refrigerate several hours to blend flavors.

NOTITA: *Use as garnish or as salad dressing for Potato Salad (page 106).*

# Salsa de Mango

## Mango Salsa

Makes 6 to 8 servings

*Mangos, green and rosy on the outside and brilliant orange inside, are one of the most luscious fruits in the world. Their sweet and slightly salty taste and creamy texture are totally quenching when eaten raw out of hand and blend well with other fruits. Here we make a salsa that marries them with tomatoes, onions and chile. It's like nothing else in the world.*

**2 mangos, or 1 jar mangos, peeled, diced and puréed**

**3 tomatoes chopped**

**1/4 cup minced onion**

**1 tablespoon white vinegar**

**1 cup finely chopped fresh Anaheim chile, roasted, page 10**

Combine all ingredients in a glass bowl and blend well. Cover and chill.

**NOTITA:** *This salsa is perfect with chicken or pork.*

# Salsa de Chile Colorado

## Red Enchilada Sauce

Makes about 2 quarts

*The French have their Mother Velouté (basic white sauce) and Mexicans have Salsa de Chile Colorado.*

**12 dried red chiles**

**2 qt. water, boiling**

**3 tablespoons oil**

**1/4 cup garlic purée, page 12**

**1/2 teaspoon salt, or to taste**

**3 tablespoons flour**

Rinse chiles in cold water and remove stems. Cook in boiling water until tender, about 15 minutes. Remove chiles and reserve the cooking liquid.

Place a few of the chiles in a blender or food processor with 1/2 cup reserved liquid, and blend to a paste. Remove to bowl. Repeat with remaining chiles.

Heat oil in a large skillet. Add garlic purée and flour, stirring until flour browns. Add the chile paste, stirring constantly until it boils and thickens. Season with salt. Thin slightly with cooking liquid.

## Salsa Adobo

### Chile Paste

Makes 2 quarts

This rich red paste is the starting place for many good-tasting recipes. Thinned with a cooking liquid, such as chicken broth, it becomes a sauce for enchiladas and other dishes. Unthinned, with vinegar or herbs added, it is called *adobado*. Adobado is a wonderful marinade for beef or pork (see page 84).

**12 dried red chiles**

**2 qt. water, boiling**

Rinse chiles in cold water and remove stems. Cook in boiling water until tender, about 15 minutes. Remove chiles and reserve the cooking liquid.

Place a few of the chiles in a blender or food processor with 1/2 cup reserved liquid, and blend to a paste. Remove to bowl. Repeat with remaining chiles.

## Real Secret Sauce

Salsa de Chile Colorado is used in countless Mexican dishes. It is available canned and is usually called **enchilada sauce**. But nothing commercial is as good as the sauce you make yourself from dried red chile peppers. That is the **real** secret sauce. And it doesn't come canned. If you do nothing else from scratch, at least make your own Salsa de Chile Colorado.

# Salsa para Tacos

## Taco Sauce

Makes 1 quart

*Basic tomato salsa for tacos can be made picante (hot) by adding 4 crushed dried de árbol chile peppers.*

*Taco sauce is the basic sauce used for tacos, tostadas and as a salad dressing.*

1 (16 oz.) canned crushed tomatoes

1 cup canned tomato purée, or substitute $^1/_2$ cup canned tomato paste mixed with $^1/_2$ cup water

1 cup water

$^1/_2$ medium white onion, chopped

$^1/_4$ cup garlic purée, page 12

$^1/_2$ cup oil

$^1/_4$ cup vinegar

4 tablespoons dried leaf oregano

1 teaspoon salt, or to taste

4 de árbol chiles, crushed (optional)

Mix all ingredients in saucepan. Bring to the boil and turn off heat. Cool. Taste and adjust seasoning. Can be served hot or cold. Refrigerate up to one week.

# Salsa Jalapeño

## Hot Jalapeño Sauce

Makes about 2 cups

*This sizzling sauce is especially good with brunch or dinner egg dishes.*

*Moderating the heat on this one is difficult, just because of the nature of jalapeños. Even decreasing the ratio of jalapeños to tomatoes will give you a fire-hot salsa.*

*For a different taste, try substituting one tablespoon lime juice in place of the salt.*

$^1/_2$ cup water

$^1/_2$ cup chopped white onion

$^1/_4$ cup garlic purée, page 12

2 tomatoes, peeled and chopped

12 jalapeños, seeded and chopped

$^1/_2$ teaspoon salt

Place water in nonstick skillet and add onion, garlic and tomato. Cook until soft. Transfer to blender. Add jalapeños and salt (or lime juice) and blend until all ingredients are smooth.

**NOTITA:** *Wear vinyl gloves when handling chiles. The oils can irritate sensitive skin.*

# Salsa Verde del Mercado

## Simple Green Sauce

**Makes about 3 cups**

*One morning while I was roaming the Los Angeles Grand Central Market, I saw a woman dicing green chiles and dropping them into a blender with a cup of broth. She heated the concoction, tasted, added salt, and there it was: Green Sauce. So simple, so good, and wonderful to cook with. It's excellent for enchiladas.*

**2 cups chopped fresh Anaheim chiles, roasted, page 10**

**1 cup chicken broth**

**Salt to taste**

Place chile and broth in blender and blend until smooth. Pour into saucepan and heat slowly over medium heat. Bring to the boil, then reduce heat and simmer 10 minutes. Taste and add salt. Cool. Cover and refrigerate.

# Salsa Verde para Enchiladas

## Green Enchilada Sauce

**Makes about 3 cups**

*I like to use a more complicated sauce, like this one, for baking chicken breasts. I serve them topped with more sauce, chopped tomatoes and crumbly Mexican cheese. Then I return the dish to the oven until the sauce is bubbly. No tortillas here—serve with crusty French bread.*

**2 tablespoons vegetable oil**

**$^1/_2$ white onion, chopped**

**2 tablespoons flour**

**2 cups chopped Anaheim chiles, page 10**

**$^1/_4$ cup garlic purée, page 12**

**2 cups chicken stock (or use bouillon cubes)**

**$^3/_4$ teaspoon salt, or to taste**

In a medium skillet, heat oil and sauté onion. Add the flour and mix well. Stir in the chiles, garlic purée, stock and salt and simmer 20 minutes. Purée in blender. Use immediately as a warm sauce for enchiladas. Or refrigerate or freeze for later use.

**NOTITA:** *A beautiful plate can be made by saucing one part of a dish with green salsa and the other with red.*

# Meats, Poultry and Fish

## Carnes, Pollo y Pescado

*Never-ending variations in preparation, spicing, saucing and serving are what keep true chefs like Monica cooking. It's an art that is infinite as composing music or wielding a paint brush, tuning an engine or building a house. It is this undefinable art that fascinated my aunt and now fascinates me.*

*Meat fillings for tacos and tamales, for burritos and sandwiches can be viewed as all the same—like the paint stroke on a canvas. They can be savored as much for their singularity as for their multiplicity. Basically, any cut of beef or pork, goat, chicken or turkey can be slowly simmered in liquid and cut or pulled apart, producing an important component of Mexican food: shredded meat.*

*That's textbook. Now for the art: Freedom! Whimsy! Paint with sauces; tune with spices. A meal is your own creation, according to your own taste.*

*Here are recipes for some of the ways I prepare meat. Take it from there.*

**NOTITA:** *In the restaurant, of course, we strive for consistency so you can come back to order the exact taste sensation you had before. At home, I wouldn't think of it (except for traditional occasions)!*

**Photo on pages 68-69: left to right—Picadillo, Bistec Ranchera, Barbacoa**

# Beef

## Tacos

Tacos are snack foods in Mexico, but in the States we often make a meal of them.

You will see tacos prepared in several ways. Some cooks use a pre-fried, U-shaped corn tortilla shell. Tacos at El Charro are sometimes rolled and sometimes folded, but always fried after they are filled, not before. A variation is called a *flauta,* which we make by placing two tightly rolled, fried tacos end to end, garnishing them with Guacamole (page 19), on one end and sour cream on the other.

Many kinds of cooked and shredded meat, fish, and poultry or beans are used to fill tacos, including one of the easiest fillings, ground beef.

## Carne Seca

Jerked or dried meat is another ancient food that has a place in the modern world. These days jerky is prized for its taste alone. Originally, of course, jerky was made by drying meat over fire and smoke so it could be kept without spoiling. In the drying process, the product was concentrated, providing great food value for its bulk and weight.

I believe most of the jerked meat available in this country is made from beef and served in Mexican restaurants. It is called *carne seca,* dry meat.

## An Alternative

We have developed a recipe that enables anyone to create a reasonable facsimile of carne seca. It's called *Machaca* and it means "hacked-up dried meat" (page 72).

Making machaca is a three-step process: You cook the beef and pull it apart; then you dry it in a 300°F (150°C) oven; and finally you fry the dried meat in a little oil with fresh onions, tomatoes, green chiles, garlic and other ingredients.

## Carne Seca

At El Charro, carne seca is our specialty. We produce it with much exertion—including aerial dramatics.

Now that we have added the historic property next door, converted it into our colorful and comfortable cocktail lounge, *!Toma¡*, and taken over the brick patio in between, our guests can see the acrobatics my husband goes through to bring them carne seca.

He engineered a steel cage in which to dry the meat and to keep it safe from predators of various sizes and predilections. These days we use four cages to keep up with demand at all our locations. They sway in the wind above the patio, off El Charro's south-facing roof.

This is a great improvement over Monica's method of hanging meat to dry. She hung strips of meat on a clothesline in a room much like a storage shed, except impeccably clean and with lots of windows. Nonetheless, the room reeked of garlic.

Every day Ray oversees the hoisting of fifty pounds of beef strips up a pole to dry in the sun. After several hours, he sees that it is brought down. The meat is shredded, then spiced and sautéed.

Carne seca is our specialty, and the recipe has been requested frequently throughout the years. However, our process for making carne seca cannot be duplicated in a home kitchen so we suggest an alternative.

# Tacos de Carne

*Beef Tacos*

**Makes 12 tacos**

*You will note the canned peas in this and other recipes. There is no excuse for them, except that's what Monica used, so that's what I use.*

*Note the egg: It binds the meat into a mini meat loaf.*

**2 cups oil for deep frying**

**$^1/_2$ cup flour**

**$^1/_2$ teaspoon salt, or to taste**

**$^1/_2$ teaspoon ground black pepper**

**$^1/_4$ cup garlic purée, page 12**

**1 egg**

**1 lb. lean ground beef**

**12 corn tortillas**

**GARNISH:**

**1 cup shredded green cabbage**

**4 cups shredded lettuce**

**2 cups Taco Sauce, page 64**

**$^1/_2$ cup sliced radishes**

**$^1/_2$ cup canned peas, drained**

**$^1/_2$ lb. shredded longhorn cheese, or other cheese**

Heat oil in a deep fryer or saucepan to 375°F (190°C). Work the flour, salt, pepper, garlic purée and egg into the beef. Warm the tortillas if they are not pliable enough. Spread 2 tablespoons beef mixture on one half of a tortilla. Fold over, press lightly and secure with wooden pick. Repeat with remaining tortillas. Fry in hot oil until crisp. Drain on paper towels. Remove picks and open tacos, while they are still hot, and quickly stuff with shredded cabbage and lettuce and a tablespoon of taco sauce. Garnish with radishes and peas and sprinkle generously with cheese.

**LOW-FAT NOTITA:** *By using ground turkey and egg substitute you can lower the fat content considerably.*

**NOTITA:** *Shredded, pulled beef, like Machaca (page 72), also works well in tacos. Because the meat is precooked, these tacos can be baked instead of fried.*

# Machaca

## Carne Seca Substitute

**Makes 8 to 12 servings**

*Making carne seca at El Charro requires special equipment—and Tucson's sun. It cannot be duplicated at home. But machaca is close!*

*Meat prepared this way has endless uses as fillings for burros, chimichangas, enchiladas, chalupas and almost any dish that calls for shredded or flaked, strongly spiced meat.*

**3 qt. water**

**$^1/_4$ cup garlic purée, page 12**

**4- to 6-lb. roast of beef (eye of round, brisket or chuck), cut into several pieces**

TO BROWN AND DRY MEAT:

**Juice of 2 limes**

**$^1/_4$ cup garlic purée, page 12**

TO FRY MEAT:

**$^1/_3$ cup oil**

**Shredded and roasted meat from above**

**1 cup chopped fresh Anaheim chiles, roasted, page 10**

**$^1/_2$ teaspoon salt, or to taste**

**$^1/_2$ teaspoon ground black pepper**

**$^1/_2$ white onion, sliced into rings**

**2 tomatoes, chopped**

**$^1/_4$ cup garlic purée, page 12**

In an 8-quart stock pot, bring water to the boil. Add $^1/_4$ cup garlic purée and meat, and return to the boil. Skim off froth, reduce heat and simmer about 2 hours, or until meat is tender, removing froth as needed. Drain juices and reserve. Remove meat and set aside until cool enough to handle. With fingers, shred meat along the grain into $^1/_2$-inch-wide strips.

Combine lime juice and $^1/_4$ cup garlic purée. Preheat oven to 325°F (165°C). Spread shredded meat in a single layer on a large cookie sheet and sprinkle with lime juice mixed with garlic purée. Roast meat until brown and as dry as you choose, at least 15 minutes, and up to an hour, stirring occasionally.

**NOTITA:** *At this point, you may cool, cover and refrigerate or freeze the meat for later use.*

Heat oil in a large skillet. Sauté chile with salt and pepper. Add onion and tomatoes and sauté briefly, then add garlic purée. Add meat, stirring over medium heat to brown. If too dry, add some reserved juices.

**NOTITA:** *Any broth left over after simmering meat, poultry or fish, which is not too highly flavored with garlic or salt, can be reduced and saved. I like to reduce the juices until they are almost like syrup and freeze them in $^1/_4$-cup containers for use in soups or sauces.*

# Barbacoa

## Barbecued Beef

Makes 6 to 8 servings

A rich and fragrant shredded beef infused with the most delicate of spices. Delicious with grilled corn on the cob as an accompaniment.

MEAT:

2 qt. water

3 lb. roast of beef (eye of round or brisket), cut into 12 pieces

$1/4$ cup garlic purée, page 12

$1^1/4$ oz. pickling spice*, tied in cheesecloth pouch

1 teaspoon salt

BARBECUE SAUCE:

4 tablespoons oil

$1/2$ cup chopped fresh Anaheim chiles, roasted, page 10

1 white onion, chopped

$1/4$ cup garlic purée, page 12

1 tablespoon vinegar

1 cup reserved meat broth

1 (8 oz.) can jalapeños, drained, thinly sliced

1 tablespoon juice from canned jalapeños

1 bay leaf

$1/2$ cup Salsa de Chile Colorado, page 63

1 teaspoon ground black pepper

$1/2$ cup green olives, minced

4 large tomatoes, chopped

$1/2$ cup wine

*Pickling spice is available commercially, in a jar or box, but you can make your own easily. To make your own bouquet garni, combine in the cheesecloth pouch: cloves, cinnamon-stick pieces, whole coriander seed, bay leaf, peppercorns and other whole spices or herbs that appeal to you.

In an 8-quart stock pot, bring water to the boil, add meat, garlic purée, spice pouch and salt. Bring to the boil again, skim froth, reduce heat and simmer 1 hour, or until the meat is tender, removing froth as it accumulates. Remove meat and let it cool enough to handle. Discard spice pouch; reserve liquid. Shred the meat by pulling apart the fibers with your fingers.

In a large skillet, heat oil and sauté green chile, onion, garlic purée, vinegar, broth and jalapeño. Add bay leaf. Add shredded meat and the remaining ingredients. Simmer about 10 minutes. Remove and discard bay leaf.

Place seasoned meat in a large, shallow baking pan and bake at 300°F (150°C) about 1 hour, stirring occasionally.

## Party Food

At weddings, showers, saints'-days celebrations and other special occasions, a hostess is sure to serve small tortillas or gorditas (which are fatter, más gordas, than flour tortillas). One is filled with beans, the other with Barbacoa, along with shredded cabbage dressed with vinegar and oil and a salsa of some kind. Often nacatamales (cocktail-size tamales), perhaps filled with chicken, potato, raisins and olives, make up part of the plate offered. And no party is complete without at least one verse of "Las Mañanitas," the Mother's Day and birthday song.

Bizcochuelos (page 120), buttery cookies shaped like wreaths, with the unforgettable flavor of anise, are expected for dessert.

## Barbecue Means Fiesta

Say "barbecue" and I hear "fiesta!"

Food for a Mexican-American fiesta is always prepared by more than one cook. An experienced cook within the family, usually a woman, gathers a troop of eager novices (maybe some not so eager) into the kitchen. Depending on her character, she'll be a drill sergeant or a patient mentor. Either way, these teachers never do this honorable chore without love and respect for both the food and their apprentices.

Children are always welcomed into kitchens, whether their mothers or nanas are just sorting beans or making a flan. But at fiesta time, older children are especially welcome.

The lively ambiance of stories, reprimands and praise, and the joy of accomplishment all together in one chaotic feast preparation must be as old as woman. Traditional recipes at those moments are being passed from one generation to the next. Inevitably, each young person brings to each dish his or her own personality, an adaptation, a suggestion from a spouse or offspring, a new technique or improved equipment to a recipe. But all of them will retain the precious kitchen secrets learned while they were novices.

Photo on pages 74-75: left to right—Arroz con Fruta, Chuletas de Puerco con Aceitunas y Naranjas, Puerco con Mango

# Carne Verde

## Green Chile and Beef Stew

Carne Verde is my favorite way to eat beef—other than a charcoal-broiled Porterhouse steak. I like to think that this dish brings out the Irish in me. After all, it's just beef-and-potato stew.

**FOR MEAT AND BROTH:**

3 lb. rousl of beef (eye of round, brisket or chuck), cut into 12 pieces

3 qt. water

1 tablespoon salt, or to taste

1 tablespoon ground black pepper

1 medium white onion, quartered

**FOR STEW:**

$^1/_2$ cup oil

1 medium white onion, sliced

2 tablespoons flour

1 cup reserved broth

$^1/_4$ cup garlic purée, page 12

8 fresh Anaheim chiles, roasted, page 10, chopped

2 large potatoes, cooked, peeled and cubed

2 large tomatoes, cubed

In an 8-quart stock pot, bring water to the boil. Add meat, salt, pepper and quartered onion. Bring to the boil again and skim off froth. Lower heat and simmer 2 hours, or until meat is tender, removing froth frequently. Remove meat and let it cool enough to handle. Reserve broth.

To assemble stew: Cut cooled meat into $^1/_2$-inch pieces, removing fat.

**NOTITA:** At this point the meat may be refrigerated, along with chiles and cooked potatoes, until needed. When it is cold you can scrape off and discard the fat that congeals on top.

In a large skillet, heat oil and sauté sliced onion until soft but not brown. Stir in meat, a little at a time. Add garlic purée, stir and simmer on low. Meanwhile, dissolve flour in a small amount of reserved broth, then combine with remaining cup of broth and add to meat.

Gently fold in chiles, potatoes and tomatoes and simmer until bubbling. Taste and adjust seasoning.

**NOTITA:** This is a basic meat preparation that we serve in bowls along with tortillas, on combination plates or as filling for burros, chimis and chalupas. To stretch the meat—or to cut down on the amount of meat you eat—serve stew over rice or noodles.

# Bistec Ranchero de mi Amiguita

*Flank Steak with Peppers and Cilantro*

Makes 4 to 6 servings

*The brown rice served with this succulent beef stew was what first attracted me to it.*

*1/2 cup oil*

*2 lb. beef flank steak, cut crosswise into 1/2-inch slices*

*1 onion, sliced*

*1 tablespoon garlic purée, page 12*

*1 cup fresh Anaheim chile, roasted, page 10, diced*

*1 cup chopped tomato*

*1/2 cup chopped red bell pepper*

*1/2 cup chopped green bell pepper*

*1/2 cup chopped cilantro*

GARNISH:

*Pimiento-stuffed olives*

*Sliced apple*

Heat oil in large skillet. Sauté steak, onion, garlic purée and chile. Cook, stirring until steak is lightly browned; add tomatoes, peppers and cilantro. Season with salt and pepper.

Cover and simmer until meat is tender, about 45 minutes.

Serve over brown rice with salad on the side.

## Cilantro

Our family did not include cilantro in Tucson-style Mexican food until recently. (In fact, I still don't use it much.) Cilantro-studded food is an influence California Hispanics have had on us in Arizona. Actually, you'll probably find more cilantro in nouvelle French restaurants than in Mexican ones. Cilantro, also called **coriander**, is an important ingredient in some Asian cuisines, as well as in certain parts of Mexico and Latin America. It may be one of those culturally exchanged delights that came about as Mexico was populated by peoples from all over the world.

# Carne de Res Estilo del Rancho

*Beef Pot Roast Simmered in Coffee*

Makes 8 to 10 servings

*Marinate this roast 24 hours in wine, vinegar and onions before simmering in a rich coffee brew.*

*6 lb. beef roast (bottom round, sirloin tip, eye)*

*6 cloves garlic, peeled, cut lengthwise into slivers*

MARINADE:

*1 onion, sliced*

*3/4 cup wine vinegar*

*2 cups red wine*

*2 bay leaves*

*1/4 cup chopped mint or parsley*

TO ROAST:

*2 tablespoons bacon drippings*

*2 cups strong black coffee*

*1 cup red wine*

*1 cup water*

*2 bay leaves*

*1 lb. carrots, peeled and sliced*

*1 lb. pearl onions (boiling onions)*

*Salt and pepper to taste*

*1 lb. baby red potatoes, quartered*

GRAVY:

*2 tablespoons cornstarch*

*1/3 cup water*

With the tip of a sharp knife, make slits in beef roast and insert slivers of garlic. In a medium bowl lined with a large plastic food bag, combine marinade ingredients and meat. Pour vinegar and wine over meat in the bag. Tie the plastic bag closed. Place bowl containing bagged meat in refrigerator 24 to 36 hours, rotating the bag at least 3 times.

About 3 hours before serving, remove meat from marinade and pat dry. Discard marinade.

Heat bacon drippings in Dutch oven. Add meat and brown slowly.

Remove browned meat; discard oil. Return meat to Dutch oven, add coffee, wine, 1 cup water and bay leaves. Bring to the boil; reduce heat immediately, cover and simmer for 3 hours.

Add carrots, pearl onions and potatoes during last hour of cooking, or prepare separately to be served with roast.

To serve: Remove meat, slice and arrange on warmed platter. Remove vegetables and keep warm.

Dissolve cornstarch in water. Stir into pan juices and thicken gravy as desired. Season with salt and pepper to taste.

Arrange vegetables around sliced meat and spoon some of the gravy over them. Pass remaining gravy.

**Variation:** Serve with Christmas Mashed Potatoes, (page 53), instead of boiled potatoes. Vary the vegetables: Brussels sprouts, turnips, red or green cabbage, steamed corn on the cob, squash or asparagus in season.

# Red Chile

In our vernacular, *chile con carne* means beef with red chile sauce, nothing else; hence we refer to the dish in cooking shorthand as *Chile Colorado— Red Chile.*

# Chile Colorado/ Chile con Carne

## *Red Chile and Beef Stew*

**Makes 6 to 8 servings**

*Chile Colorado is the dish by which you can judge the quality of a Mexican restaurant. It's basic. Good-quality beef (sometimes pork, or even both) are simmered in the most Mexican of all sauces, Red Chile Sauce, the making of which is an art.*

**3-lb. roast of beef (eye of round, chuck or brisket); or half boneless pork roast**

**1 cup flour**

**1 tablespoon salt, or to taste**

**1 teaspoon ground black pepper**

**$^1/_2$ cup oil**

**3 cups Salsa de Chile Colorado, page 63**

**1 tablespoon garlic purée, page 12**

**1 teaspoon dried oregano**

Cut meat into $^3/_4$-inch pieces and place, a handful at a time, into a paper bag containing flour, salt and pepper. Shake well. Repeat with remaining meat.

In a large skillet, heat oil. Add meat, a batch at a time so the skillet is not crowded, and brown slowly. Add Salsa de Chile Colorado, garlic purée and oregano. Cook over low heat 1 hour or longer, until meat is tender, stirring frequently to prevent scorching. Add a little hot water if necessary.

# Picadillo
## Hash

**Makes 6 to 8 servings**

*This handsome, easy-to-eat ground-beef dish makes a superb filling for Chalupas (page 26) and Empanadas (page 82).*

$^1/_2$ *teaspoon salt*

$^1/_4$ *cup water*

*2 lb. lean chopped or ground beef*

$^1/_4$ *cup garlic purée, page 12*

$^1/_2$ *white onion, chopped*

*2$^1/_2$ cups diced cooked potato*

*2 celery ribs, chopped*

*1 medium tomato, peeled and diced*

$^1/_4$ *cup raisins, soaked in hot water until plump*

*8 tablespoons vinegar*

$^1/_2$ *cup ketchup mixed with $^1/_2$ cup water (optional)*

*6 green olives, pitted and chopped*

*1 to 2 teaspoons sugar (optional)*

*1 teaspoon cinnamon*

*1 cup diced unpeeled apple*

Heat skillet and add salt, water and ground beef. Stir and separate beef and brown it quickly. Add garlic purée, onion, potato, celery, tomato, raisins, vinegar, ketchup, olives, sugar, cinnamon and apples. Cook until flavors blend, about 15 minutes, stirring frequently.

**NOTITA:** *Use Spanish green olives or no olives in this recipe. Ketchup sweetens Picadillo; so, if the apples are tart, you might choose to add a little.*

## Wedding Feasts

Mexican weddings have a lot of tradition—traditions that change with time and with region and family.

Usually there is an older couple who serve as the **padrinos** or best man and best woman. They have specific duties, depending on the needs and wishes of the couple and their families. They may order and buy the wedding cake, offer toasts, give parties, and maybe even act as coordinator between the families.

There are bridesmaids and junior bridesmaids—usually all cousins—and groomsmen. There are two ring bearers. One "holds" the rings. The second bearer carries the Golden Money Box, *la Cajita de Arras*, containing coins that ensure the couple always has money for a loaf of bread.

Catholic weddings take place in church, but the reception can be at home or in a hall. There is usually a fiesta after the Mass and lots of food, drink and music. There is cake and champagne.

One dish in particular that is always prepared for a Mexican wedding is **picadillo**, chopped up little pieces of meat and potato with sweet and savory spices. In a word: hash. I don't know why it has become such a tradition. But since it has, everyone expects it and therefore it creates its own welcome for strangers and family alike. It makes everyone feel at home and is not costly to prepare. Very appropriate for a young couple—no matter who's giving the party.

*Photo on pages 80-81: Combination plate—Taco de Carne, Chalupa, Tamales de Elote, Arroz Estilo El Charro, Carne Seca, El Charro Frijoles, mini chimi, Ensalada Elegante de Guacamole (center), Salsa de Tomatillo Cruda (side dish)*

# Empanadas de Carne

## Beef Turnovers

**Makes 28 to 30 empanadas**

*A flavorful meat filling lies within these handsome turnovers. Enjoy them warmed. They make a great addition to a picnic supper.*

**MEAT FILLING:**

**2 lb. lean ground beef**

**$^1/_2$ cup raisins**

**$^1/_4$ cup sugar**

**1 teaspoon ground cinnamon**

**1 teaspoon salt**

**1 teaspoon garlic purée, page 12**

**$^1/_2$ teaspoon chopped piñon nuts or pecans**

**EMPANADA PASTRY:**

**3 cups flour**

**1 teaspoon baking powder**

**3 tablespoons chilled shortening**

**1 egg, beaten**

**1 cup ice water**

Preheat oven to 400°F (205°C).

Meat filling: Brown meat in large skillet over medium heat, stirring and breaking apart meat so that it browns evenly. Add remaining ingredients, mixing well over medium heat. If too dry, add a few tablespoons water.

Set aside to cool while preparing Empanada Pastry.

**NOTITA:** *This basic, rich pastry can be made ahead, refrigerated or frozen. If you want a less-rich pastry, omit the egg and adjust the liquid.*

Empanada pastry: Combine dry ingredients in large bowl. Cut in shortening with pastry blender or two knives until dough is consistency of coarse meal. Add beaten egg, mixing just until blended. Slowly add enough chilled water, mixing now with your hands, until dough wants to form a ball. (Over-mixing or allowing your hands to heat up the dough will make the dough tough. If necessary, chill dough before handling further.)

On a well-floured surface, roll out dough to $^1/_4$ to $^1/_2$ inch thick. Cut out circles with biscuit cutter or rim of drinking glass, 2$^1/_2$ to 3 inches in diameter.

Fill each circle with 1 tablespoonful of meat mixture. Fold in half, making a half-circle, and crimp edges to seal in the filling.

Place filled empanadas on ungreased cookie sheet and bake in preheated oven for 15 to 20 minutes or until browned. Serve immediately or rewarm later.

# Pork

When entertaining guests, I like to serve pork, which is just as traditional as beef or chicken. By offering traditional foods like these, coupled with rich spices, you will make any guest feel at home and special at the same time.

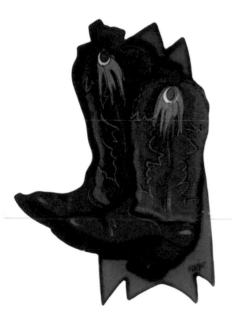

# Chuletas de Puerco con Aceitunas y Naranjas

## Pork Chops with Olives and Oranges

......................................
### Makes 6 servings
......................................

*This special-occasion dish calls for the very best trimmed, thick, center-cut pork chops.*

6 center-cut pork chops

2 tablespoons oil

1 onion chopped

1 cup beef or chicken broth

1 cup orange juice

$^1/_2$ teaspoon dried oregano

2 tablespoons garlic purée, page 12

Salt and pepper

1 (6 oz.) jar pimiento-stuffed Spanish olives, drained

1 tablespoon corn starch

2 tablespoons cold water

2 cups orange sections

Rinse and pat dry pork chops. Trim excess fat.

Heat oil in large skillet and brown chops evenly over medium heat. Remove chops and set aside. In same skillet, brown onion. Carefully add broth, orange juice, oregano, garlic purée and salt to taste.

Return chops to skillet; sprinkle olives over all. Cover, reduce heat to simmer and cook about 45 minutes, until tender. Add more broth or water as needed.

...................................
**NOTITA:** *A temperature that is too high tends to toughen pork chops; too low and they dry out.*
...................................

In small bowl or 1-cup measure, stir cornstarch into cold water and stir into sauce in skillet. Stir constantly until sauce thickens.

Fold in orange sections. Serve, topped with olives.

# Carnitas de Puerco

## Shredded Pork

......................................
### Makes 4 to 6 servings
......................................

*Here is an all-purpose shredded meat filling. When large pieces of pork are on sale, prepare a big batch and freeze some.*

2 lb. pork loin

1 onion, cut in half

2 carrots cut into 1-inch pieces

1 whole head garlic, separated, peeled if desired

1 teaspoon salt

Rinse and pat dry pork loin. Place pork loin and remaining ingredients in large kettle with water to cover food. Bring to the boil; reduce heat and simmer about 1 hour. Remove meat to cool; reserve liquid.

When pork is cool enough to handle, shred it by pulling apart the fibers with your fingers. Carnitas freeze beautifully if you add some of the reserved cooking liquid to the freezer container to fill it completely.

# Puerco Adobado

## Pork Ribs with Red Chile

**Makes 6 servings**

Thick red-chile paste, called adobo, is usually enriched with oregano, black pepper and a dash of vinegar or lemon juice. It is used for marinating pork ribs that are to be roasted in the following manner.

**1 cup Salsa Adobo, page 63**
**³/₄ cup vinegar**
**1 teaspoon salt, or to taste**
**1 teaspoon dried oregano**
**3 lb. pork ribs**

In a small bowl combine red chile paste, vinegar, salt and oregano to make a marinade. Rub marinade into pork ribs, cover and refrigerate at least 4 hours, turning occasionally. Roast at 350°F (175°C) about 1 hour, or until tender.

# Puerco con Mango

## Pork Tenderloin with Mango

**Makes 4 to 6 servings**

A tangy fruit glaze adds extra flavor to this tender roast.

**1 pork tenderloin (2 to 3 lb.)**
**2 tablespoons flour**
**2 tablespoons garlic purée, page 12**
**1 cup mango preserves or mango chutney**
**1 cup apricot jam (or other tart jam)**
**1 tablespoon ground cinnamon**
**1 tablespoon ground nutmeg**
**Salt and pepper to taste**
**¹/₂ cup packed brown sugar**
**2 tablespoons cornstarch**
**¹/₄ cup water**
**Fresh mango slices**

Preheat oven to 450°F (230°C). Coat pork tenderloin with flour, then rub in garlic purée, salt and pepper. Place meat on a rack in a shallow roasting pan.

Blend together preserves or chutney, jam, spices and sugar. Coat meat with mixture.

Insert meat thermometer. Roast at 450°F (230°C) for 10 minutes to seal in the juices. Then lower temperature to 350°F (175°C) and continue roasting until internal temperature of meat reaches 170°F (75°C).

Remove meat to cutting board. Cut into thin slices and arrange on platter or individual plates.

Skim fat from pan juices. Dissolve cornstarch in water and stir into juice. Strain sauce, if necessary, and spoon over sliced pork when serving. Slice meat and insert mango slices.

Serve with Fruited Rice, page 47.

**NOTITA:** The sweet rice is a nice foil for the spiciness of the meat and sauce.

# Chorizo—Mexican Sausage

Chorizo is usually sold in bulk and not stuffed into sausage casings. It is used like ground beef. We like to sauté it and then scramble eggs into it and roll up the mixture in flour tortillas for breakfast burritos.

A favorite Sunday-morning brunch selection at El Charro is a mouthwatering scramble of eggs and this colorful sausage, served on a hot plate with refried beans, homestyle fried potatoes and fresh tortillas. Most of our patrons believe it is a fine way to start the week.

*Scrambled eggs with Chorizo, El Charro Frijoles Refritos*

# Chorizo

*Mexican Sausage*

**Yield: 6 pounds**

*The best part of making your own chorizo is you know it has no by-products.*

*Be sure to use ground red chile powder, not chili-powder mix.*

**6 lb. lean ground beef (or half ground pork or ground turkey)**

**2 cups white wine**

**1 cup wine vinegar**

**3 teaspoons salt**

**4 tablespoons dried oregano**

**$^1/_2$ cup garlic purée, page 12**

**8 oz. ground red chile powder**

**2 qt. Salsa Adobo, page 63**

Combine ground meat, wine and vinegar thoroughly. Add salt, oregano and garlic purée. Add ground red chile powder gradually, kneading it in with your hands. Gradually knead in the chile paste. Place in large ceramic bowl, cover with plastic and refrigerate overnight. Drain any liquid. Use in a day or two, or divide into meal-size portions and freeze.

**NOTITA:** *Wear vinyl gloves when kneading this mixture; otherwise you'll have orange fingernails for a day or two.*

# Albóndigas de Chorizo

*Sweet-and-Sour Chorizo Meatballs*

**Makes 24 meatballs**

*These are very adaptable. They can be made cocktail-size and served with your favorite barbecue sauce, added to soups or stews or served plain as a meat course with rice or fried potatoes.*

**2 lb. lean ground beef**

**$1^1/_2$ lb. chorizo, opposite**

**1 slice of bread moistened in water**

**1 egg**

**$^1/_4$ teaspoon salt**

**$^1/_4$ teaspoon ground black pepper**

**$^1/_4$ cup chopped onion**

**$^1/_2$ cup pineapple jam, heated to thin**

Preheat oven to 350°F (175°C). Lightly spray a cookie sheet with cooking oil. Mix beef, chorizo, moistened bread, egg, salt, pepper, onion and pineapple jam until well blended.

Form walnut-size balls and place on prepared cookie sheet.

Bake about 10 minutes, or until cooked through.

**NOTITA:** *I like to turn the meatballs once halfway through baking so that tops and bottoms are nicely browned. After cooling a few minutes, they can be refrigerated and used later in several ways.*

**Variation:** Meatballs can be heated and served in any barbecue sauce. I like to add 1 cup of El Charro's Red Enchilada Sauce, page 63, to a barbecue sauce and paste of chipotle chiles for extra zing.

I also like to add about six links of andouille sausage, cut into chunks and pan-grilled with red and green bell peppers and onions. I toss that in with a bowl of meatballs. I serve this dish warm with crusty French bread or *bolillos,* Mexican French-style rolls.

**Low-fat variation:** Lower-fat chorizo balls can be made with ground turkey breast.

# Poultry

For many, chicken is truly the only white meat because it's easy to prepare, cooks quickly and is adaptable to a number of flavors. Relatively low-fat, chicken holds a special place in many gourmets' hearts because of its versatility.

## Pechuga de Pollo Almendrado

### Chicken Encrusted with Almonds

**Makes 6 servings**

*I like to make this chicken dish at home—I can make it early in the day and bake it in a few minutes for a late dinner-for-two. It combines the subtle flavors of almonds and cilantro.*

**24 cherry tomatoes, blanched and peeled**

**¹/₂ cup tequila, divided**

**3 chicken breasts, skinned, boned, halved**

**2 tablespoons lime juice**

**1 tablespoon garlic purée, page 12**

**2 tablespoons flour**

**2 cups almonds**

**¹/₄ cup Pico de Gallo seasoning, page 13**

**Marinated cherry tomatoes, optional**

**Fresh cilantro**

**¹/₂ onion sliced**

**2 avocados, peeled and diced**

Preheat oven to 350°F (175°C).

Place blanched and peeled cherry tomatoes in bowl with half the tequila. Toss, set aside.

Place each chicken breast between sheets of waxed paper and pound to flatten slightly. Place them in a glass pie plate with remaining tequila, lime juice and garlic purée, tossing to coat well. Set aside (or cover and refrigerate for later use).

Meanwhile, prepare coating: Place flour and almonds in food processor and process until coarsely ground. Mix in Pico de Gallo and process a few seconds longer. Remove almond mixture to second pie plate or square of waxed paper.

Lightly coat a 13 x 9-inch baking pan with oil and dust it with flour.

Dip each piece of marinated chicken into almond mixture and place in prepared baking pan. At this point the dish may be held, covered and refrigerated until a half-hour before serving.

Sprinkle any leftover almond mixture over chicken and bake, uncovered, about 20 minutes, until cooked through.

Remove chicken to individual plates or a platter and garnish with marinated cherry tomatoes, cilantro, onion rings and avocado.

# Pollo Borracho

*Grilled Chicken
in Spirits*

**Makes 6 servings**

Borracho, *meaning drunk, is
a term used in Mexican cooking to describe meat that has
been marinated in beer and
seasonings.*

**6 pieces boneless, skinless
chicken breasts (1$^1$/$_2$ to 2 lb.)**

MARINADE:

**$^1$/$_4$ cup lime juice**

**$^1$/$_4$ cup oil**

**12 oz. dark-brewed Mexican or
other beer**

**2 tablespoons garlic purée,
page 12**

**2 cloves, crushed**

**1 cardamom seed, crushed**

**1 bay leaf**

**6 black peppercorns, crushed**

**$^1$/$_2$ teaspoon salt**

Rinse and pat dry chicken
breasts, trimming fat. Combine marinade ingredients in
large bowl. Add chicken
breasts, turning to coat well.
Cover, refrigerate and marinate at least 3 hours.

Remove chicken from mari-
nade and pat dry.

Grill chicken over charcoal
2 to 5 minutes per side
(depending upon thickness of
chicken) until cooked through,
brushing with marinade frequently. Slice chicken and
serve as desired.

**N○TIT A:** *Discard leftover marinade to prevent contamination.*

**Variation 1:** Pull grilled
chicken into shreds and use as
filling for tacos, enchiladas or
burros.

**Variation 2:** Pan grill or
bake the chicken rather than
charbroiling for a different
taste. Don't overcook.

**Variation 3: Chicken
Quesadilla**

Thinly slice cooked chicken
breast (grilled is best-tasting)
and place on fresh tortilla.
Cover with thin slices or
crumbles of Mexican cheese.
Top with another tortilla.
Lightly butter a skillet. Over
medium heat, cook the quesadilla, flipping once, until
cheese melts. Cut into wedges
and serve as main course with
beans and salad or as appetizer with salsa.

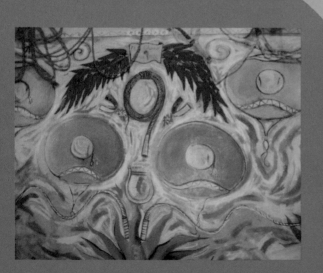

# Tacos de Pollo

## Chicken Tacos

**Makes 12 chicken tacos**

*Sometimes we bake tacos instead of frying them. At El Charro we never use any part of the chicken except the breast* (la pechuga).

**12 corn tortillas**

**2 cups oil, warmed**

**2 cups poached, shredded chicken breast meat**

**Salt and pepper to taste**

GARNISH:

**1 cup shredded green cabbage or lettuce**

**4 cups shredded lettuce (variety)**

**1 cup canned peas**

**$^{1}/_{2}$ cup sliced radishes**

**4 cups (1 lb.) white, crumbly Mexican-style cheese or longhorn cheese, shredded, or other cheese**

**2 cups Taco Sauce, page 64**

Dip each tortilla in warm oil and place on a cookie sheet. Place about 2 tablespoons of the seasoned, shredded chicken at one end of a tortilla. Roll the tortilla around the filling and secure with a wooden pick. Repeat with remaining tortillas.

**NOTITA:** *It is important to keep tortillas from drying out when working with them by covering them with a damp towel.*

Heat remaining oil to deep-frying temperature and then place tacos, two at a time, in the oil, turning them until they are brown on all sides. Drain on paper towels. Remove picks and serve on a platter and garnish with cabbage, lettuce, peas, radishes, cheese and Taco Sauce.

**Variation:** To bake tacos rather than fry them, place tacos on tray in preheated 350°F (175°C) oven. Turn 2 or 3 times to brown tacos evenly.

**LOW-FAT NOTITA:** *Warming corn tortillas in the microwave for a few seconds makes them pliable enough to roll, so there is really no need to dip them in hot oil before forming.*

*Photo on pages 90-91: left to right—Topopo, Pollo Borracho, Las Charras Enchiladas de Pollo*

# Las Charras Enchiladas de Pollo

## Rolled Enchiladas with Chicken

**Makes 12 enchiladas**

*Chicken enchiladas are one of our most popular dishes. We serve them for brunch, lunch or dinner.*

1 qt. water

4 large chicken breasts

2 cups oil

12 corn tortillas

2 qt. Salsa de Chile Colorado, page 63

4 cups (1 lb.) longhorn or jack cheese, shredded

GARNISH:

1 avocado, pitted, peeled and sliced

2 cups sour cream, optional

In an 8-quart stock pot bring water to the boil. Add chicken breasts, bring to the boil again, reduce heat and simmer 20 minutes, or until chicken is tender. Drain and cool. Discard skin and bones. Shred meat and set aside, covered with a damp towel.

Preheat oven to 350°F (175°C). In a large skillet, heat oil. Dip each tortilla in oil and place on waxed paper. Place 2 tablespoons chicken in the center of each tortilla and roll each loosely. Place seam side down and side by side in a shallow baking dish. Cover with Salsa de Chile Colorado and a blanket of shredded cheese. Bake in preheated oven until bubbly, about 10 minutes. Garnish with avocado slices and sour cream, if using.

# Pollo en Pipián

## Chicken with Pumpkin Seeds and Red Chile Sauce

**Makes 6 servings**

*This dish is usually served with Enchiladas Sonorenses, page 27, so that the diner can sample two types of chile sauce: red, made from dried red chiles, and Pipián, made from pumpkin seeds and tasting a lot like peanuts.*

*Of course, you could save time by purchasing Pipián sauce that's available in Southwestern and Asian markets.*

*If you like the peanut flavor in the Pipián sauce, then omit the pumpkin seeds altogether and substitute several teaspoons peanut butter for the pumpkin-seed paste and almonds.*

**CHICKEN:**

**6 chicken breasts (or 3 whole breasts split)**

**1 qt. water**

**PIPIÁN SAUCE:**

**4 dried red chiles**

**1 qt. water**

**$^1/_2$ cup dry pumpkin seeds, shelled**

**$^1/_2$ cup blanched almonds**

**1 slice bread, toasted and cubed**

**$^1/_4$ cup garlic purée, page 12**

**3 cups strained reserved chicken broth (below)**

**$^1/_3$ cup sherry**

**2 teaspoons heated oil (microwave oil in small glass dish for a few seconds)**

**Salt, to taste**

Chicken: Poach chicken breasts in 1 quart water until cooked through, about 20 minutes. Remove chicken and set aside to cool enough to handle. Reserve chicken broth. Carefully remove and discard skin and bones from chicken, leaving breasts whole.

Pipián Sauce: Discard stems from red chiles; wash and soak chiles in 1 quart water 15 minutes. Drain.

In a dry skillet, toast together the pumpkin seeds and almonds, shaking pan continually until the seeds and nuts are lightly browned. Do not burn.

Place toasted seeds and nuts in blender with soaked and drained chiles, toasted bread, and garlic purée. Blend to a paste. It will be slightly gritty. Scrape into a large skillet; add reserved chicken broth and sherry and simmer over low heat until sauce thickens.

Remove from heat and whisk in very hot oil, drop by drop. Return to heat and cook slowly, stirring constantly until the fat comes to the surface. Salt to taste.

**NOTITA:** *Do not add salt earlier or the sauce may curdle.*

To assemble: Place cooked chicken into skillet with sauce and cook over very low heat about 15 minutes, checking often to make sure sauce is not scorching.

# Pechuga de Pollo en Pipián Rápido

## Speedy Chicken in Peanut Sauce

**Makes 4 servings**

*If you like the taste of peanuts, you'll find many uses for this ancient sauce. Here is a quick, modern version.*

**4 boneless, skinless chicken breasts**

**1¹/₂ cups peanut butter**

**1 tablespoon garlic purée, page 12**

**1 (24 oz.) can red enchilada sauce**

**1 cup canned chicken broth**

Preheat oven to 350°F (175°C). Spread chicken breasts with peanut butter and place in baking dish. Combine garlic purée with enchilada sauce and chicken broth. Pour sauce over chicken breasts. Bake in preheated oven 25 minutes, basting chicken frequently. Remove chicken to serving platter. Over high heat, reduce sauce in pan and pour over servings. Serve with El Charro Rice (page 47) and Refried Beans (page 49).

# Pollo y Fideo

## Chicken and Pasta

**Makes 6 to 8 servings**

*When we were little, our favorite television show was "I Love Lucy" on Monday nights. My mom would make this for us, so we could eat from TV trays.*

**CHICKEN:**

**3 or 4 whole chicken breasts**

**¹/₂ cup flour**

**Salt and pepper**

**Vegetable oil**

**1 (16 oz.) can whole tomatoes**

**1 (16 oz.) can tomato sauce**

**SAUCE:**

**¹/₂ lb. mushrooms, thick sliced**

**1 onion, sliced**

**1 green or red bell pepper, seeded and sliced**

**TO SERVE:**

**1 lb. fideo (vermicelli), cooked al dente**

**2 to 3 cups crumbled Mexican cheese (casero)**

**6 to 8 oz. green olives, chopped**

Rinse and pat dry chicken. Cut into serving pieces. Roll in flour seasoned with salt and pepper to taste. Shake off excess flour.

Heat large skillet over medium heat. Coat with vegetable oil. Add chicken carefully and brown. Add tomatoes and tomato sauce. Bring up to simmer, cover and cook over low heat 15 minutes, less if chicken pieces are small.

Meanwhile cook fideo in boiling water until al dente.

In another skillet coated lightly with oil, sauté onion until heated through. Add mushrooms and bell pepper and sauté briefly. Add this mixture to chicken, stirring until combined. Cover and cook over low heat 20 to 30 minutes longer or until chicken is thoroughly cooked.

Serve over cooked *fideo*. Sprinkle crumbled cheese generously over the chicken and garnish with chopped olives.

**NOTITA:** *The last cooking can be done in a 350°F (175°C) oven if that is more convenient. In that case, you may want to assemble the chicken and vegetables in a serving casserole.*

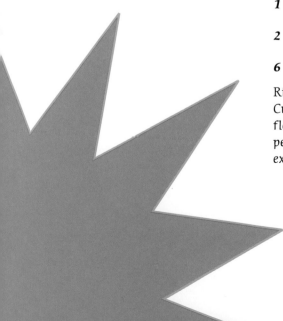

# Fish

Although substituting fish for meat during Lent is no longer mandatory, old traditions die hard. El Charro continues to observe Lent by offering a special fish platter, which often features Pescado Viscayena (page 96), on Fridays during Lent.

Every year, about four weeks before Lent begins, we start to stockpile ingredients we will need for Lenten dishes. But even more important to us is that the kitchen crew know the significance and importance of the Lenten season and its foods.

It is important for us to display for guests and educate our staff about the culture and traditions of the family—starting with our history and trickling down to our religion.

*Ceviche, with condiments (see recipe on page 105)*

# Pescado Viscayena

## *Fish Fillets with Vegetables*

**Makes 8 servings**

*You may recognize this Pescado Viscayena as Pescado Veracruzano. The two styles are similar. Capers are usually added to Veracruz style.*

**8 (6 oz. each) boneless fish fillets (cod, sole or snapper)**

**$^1/_2$ cup margarine, melted**

**Salt and pepper to taste**

**$^1/_4$ cup fresh lime juice**

**1 white onion, sliced into rings**

**SAUCE:**

**$^1/_4$ cup oil**

**2 green bell peppers, seeded, sliced into rings**

**2 or 3 potatoes, cooked, peeled and diced**

**$^1/_4$ cup lime juice**

**1 cup frozen peas and carrots**

**$^1/_2$ teaspoon Tabasco sauce**

**$^1/_2$ cup chopped white onion**

**2 tablespoons garlic purée, page 12**

**Salt and pepper to taste**

**$^1/_2$ cup fresh cilantro**

**6 Anaheim chiles, roasted, page 10, chopped**

**$^1/_4$ cup water or white wine**

**GARNISH:**

**Fresh cilantro**

**8 pieces lime**

Fish preparation: Preheat oven to 325°F (165°C). Rinse and pat fillets dry. Coat glass baking pan with melted margarine. Arrange fillets in one layer in pan. Sprinkle with salt and pepper and lime juice and scatter onion over all. Cover and bake in a preheated oven 10 to 15 minutes, depending upon thickness of fish pieces. Drain off broth and reserve to add to sauce just before serving.

Sauce preparation: Assemble and prepare sauce ingredients while fillets are baking.

Fifteen minutes before serving, combine sauce ingredients in a large skillet and bring to the boil. Cover and simmer 10 minutes. Stir in reserved fish broth.

Spoon sauce over fillets, and return to oven to finish cooking, about 10 minutes.

Serve with cilantro and lime garnish.

# Tacos de Camarón

## *Shrimp Tacos*

**Makes 12 tacos**

*Surprise your family with this version of tacos. Our guests are enthusiastic about them.*

**1 tablespoon butter or margarine**

**$^1/_2$ onion, minced**

**3 jalapeños, chopped**

**2 tomatoes, chopped**

**$^1/_4$ teaspoon garlic purée, page 12**

**Pepper to taste**

**1 lb. boiled shrimp, shelled, deveined and roughly chopped (or use small shrimp)**

**Juice of 1 lemon**

**Juice of 2 limes**

**12 corn tortillas, folded in half and lightly deep fried, page 25**

**3 cups ($^3/_4$ lb.) shredded cabbage**

**Lime wedges**

In a large skillet, sauté in butter or margarine the onion, jalapeños, tomatoes and garlic purée until heated through. Add shrimp and juices and cook 5 minutes.

Place about 2 tablespoons of filling into each tortilla taco shell.

Garnish with shredded cabbage and lime wedges.

**Variation:** You may substitute lobster or white fish pieces for the shrimp.

# Tortas Fritas de Camarón

## *Shrimp Fritters*

**Makes 12 fritters**

*When a special cocktail snack is called for, you can't do better than to serve Shrimp Fritters. Like all fried foods, serve these immediately. You can make the batter a day in advance.*

**4 eggs, separated**

**1 zucchini, grated**

**2 cups grated, cooked, peeled potato**

**4 oz. small cooked, peeled shrimp**

**4 oz. corn kernels, fresh or frozen**

**1 jalapeño, chopped**

**$^1/_2$ onion, diced**

**$^1/_2$ teaspoon garlic purée, page 12**

**Salt and pepper to taste**

**1 cup bread crumbs**

**Vegetable oil for frying**

**GARNISH:**

**Chopped tomato, chopped cucumber, lime wedges**

Beat egg whites until stiff. In another bowl, beat yolks. Gently fold beaten whites into yolks. Set aside.

Combine remaining ingredients, except bread crumbs and oil, using your hands to blend well, but with a light touch. Form patties from the mixture $^1/_2$ inch thick and about 3 inches in diameter; set aside.

Meanwhile, heat oil for frying in a deep fryer (a mini-fryer is ideal) or a deep skillet.

When oil is at correct temperature, dip each patty into egg mixture to coat thoroughly, then into bread crumbs. Carefully lower patties, one by one, into hot oil, a few at a time. Fry until golden, remove and set on paper toweling to drain.

Serve hot with a garnish of chopped tomato and cucumber and lime wedges; with cheese and salsa as a main dish. Or make smaller patties and serve them as hors d'oeuvres or a side dish, with lime wedges as garnish.

**Variation:** Substitute crab meat for the shrimp and make Desert Crab Cakes.

## Salsa para Tortas Fritas
### Sauce for Fried Seafood

Makes about $1^1/_2$ cups

*A simple salsa adds the final touch.*

**1 (8 oz.) can crushed tomatoes**

**1 (4 oz.) can chopped green chiles**

**1 teaspoon horseradish**

**Juice of 1 lemon**

**$^1/_2$ teaspoon salt**

Combine all ingredients.

# Pescado en Estilo de Enchilada
## Baked Cod, Enchilada-style

Makes 6 servings

*For a party or special dinner, garnish with garlicky, grilled shrimp. Children who don't normally like fish often like it when prepared this way.*

**6 (6 oz.) pieces boneless cod, sea bass or other firm, thick white fish**

**$^1/_4$ cup margarine**

**1 tablespoon garlic purée, page 12**

**2 cups grated Monterey jack cheese**

**2 cups grated sharp cheddar cheese**

**2 cups Anaheim chile, roasted, page 10, chopped**

**$^1/_2$ cup chopped green onion**

**2 cups yellow corn (optional)**

**18 medium shrimp, shelled and deveined**

SAUCE:

**$^1/_2$ cup garlic purée, page 12**

**3 to 4 cups Enchilada Sauce, page 63, heated**

GARNISH:

**1 cup crumbled Mexican-style cheese**

**$^1/_2$ cup chopped cilantro**

**2 or 3 limes, cut into wedges**

**2 or 3 oranges, cut into wedges**

Preheat oven to 350°F (175°C). In lightly greased baking pan, place fish in one layer. Combine margarine with garlic purée. Dot each piece using half of the garlic mixture, reserving remainder. Cover loosely with foil. Bake in preheated oven about 15 minutes, until fish is no longer translucent.

Meanwhile in a large bowl combine grated cheese, chiles, green onion and corn, if using.

Drain juices from partially cooked fish and reserve. Top each piece of fish generously with cheese mixture. Return to pan, cover and bake about 10 minutes until cheese melts.

In a large skillet, sauté shrimp in the remaining garlic margarine until warmed through and just cooked.

To serve: Heat serving platter. In sauce pan, heat garlic purée, Enchilada Sauce and reserved fish juices. Spoon some of the sauce onto the heated platter to coat it. Carefully transfer the fish and topping to the platter. Top with shrimp, Mexican cheese, cilantro and wedges of lime and orange.

*Photo on pages 98-99: From left—Tortas Fritas de Camarón, Pescado Viscayena*

# Salads

## Ensaladas

*During one of Monica Flin's excursions to Mexico, she was enchanted by the volcano Popocatépetl outside of the capital. It impressed her so much that when she returned to Tucson she created a cone-shaped salad and gave it the name* Topopo, *Indian for volcano. Further refined, it became* Topopo Jalisciense. Jalisciense *means in the style of food in the state of Jalisco, Mexico. We are not sure why "Jalisco." Maybe because* Topopo Popocatépetl *is too hard to say.*

Photo on pages 102-103: Ensalada de Espinaca

# Topopo a la Jalisciense

*Volcano Salad
Jalisco-style*

**Makes 8 servings**

*Topopos have become popular all over Tucson. They are basically a huge salad erected like an Aztec temple . . . on a tostada.*

*This recipe is easily adapted for vegetarians. It can even be made with fruit.*

**FOR TORTILLA BASE:**

**Oil for frying**

**8 corn tortillas**

**2 cups Frijoles Refritos, page 49**

**SALAD:**

**4 small romaine lettuce heads, julienned**

**2 cups frozen mixed vegetables, cooked**

**Salt to taste**

**Pepper to taste**

**1 cup Basic Vinaigrette, below**

**GARNISH:**

**4 boneless chicken breasts, poached, skinned, each cut into 8 strips**

**2 large avocados, sliced into 16 pieces**

**32 strips jack cheese**

**1 (7 oz.) jar jalapeños, drained, sliced**

**2 tomatoes, quartered**

**8 green olives, chopped**

**1 cup shredded Mexican cheese**

In a large skillet, heat oil and fry tortillas for a few seconds; set aside to drain on paper towels. In a saucepan, heat Frijoles Refritos, cover and keep warm.

**NOTITA:** *Make a double batch of the dressing and refrigerate half for later use.*

Combine lettuce with cooked vegetables, salt and pepper. Moisten with Basic Vinaigrette.

To serve each salad: Spread $1/4$ cup Frijoles Refritos on each fried tortilla. Pack 2 cups of the salad mixture into a 4-inch funnel and unmold it onto the prepared tortilla. Garnish with $1/8$ of the chicken, avocado, cheese strips and jalapeño placed vertically along the slopes of the volcano. At the summit of the Topopo, place one tomato quarter, then sprinkle with chopped olives and cheese.

Serve with additional Vinaigrette on the side.

**Variation 1:** Lately I find our guests enjoy a choice of dressings, including a vinaigrette made with raspberry- or prickly-pear-flavored vinegar.

**Variation 2:** This versatile salad can be made with cooked whole pinto beans or guacamole on the bottom.

## Basic Vinaigrette

**$1/2$ cup oil**

**$1/4$ cup white vinegar**

**Salt and pepper to taste**

Shake ingredients in covered jar, or slowly whisk oil into vinegar and seasoning.

**Variation:** Some cooks like to add a dash of sugar and a dab of strong mustard to this dressing.

**LOW-FAT NOTITA:** *Buy a small spray bottle and fill it with your favorite salad oil. When assembling your salad greens, spray them lightly with the oil and toss. You'll be amazed at how little oil is used. Then dress the salad with dressing made without additional oil.*

# Ensalada de Nopales

*Prickly Pear Salad*

**Makes 6 servings**

*Edible cactus is one of those foods that surprises many of Tucson's visitors. Canned nopalitos, available in specialty markets, may be used. Rinse and drain before adding them to the dish.*

**12 prickly-pear pads (nopales, nopalitos), cut into strips, page 11**

**6 tomatoes, chopped**

**1 large onion, chopped**

**4 jalapeños, chopped**

**$1/2$ cup chopped cilantro, optional**

**2 tablespoons vinegar**

Cook cactus pads in water to remove slippery gel. When tender, rinse pads in cold water and chop.

In glass or ceramic bowl, combine chopped *nopales* with remaining ingredients. Serve immediately on lettuce leaves, or cover and chill to enable flavors to become bolder.

**NOTITA:** *Serve Ensalada de Nopales scrambled into eggs or as a relish or side dish. See also sautéed nopales, page 56.*

# Ensalada Elegante de Guacamole

## Elegant and Chunky Avocado Salad

**Makes about 6 cups**

Guacamole is not only a succulent dip but doubles as a lovely salsa or relish for cold turkey or broiled fish. Or, serve a scoop of it in the middle of a plate of boiled shrimp and tomato slices, all on a bed of lettuce, and you have lunch.

**4 large avocados, seeded, peeled and cubed**

**4 large tomatoes, cubed**

**$1/4$ cup chopped cilantro**

**6 green onions, chopped**

**1 cup diced queso fresco**

**1 tablespoon diced green olives**

**$1/4$ cup diced cucumber or zucchini**

**1 teaspoon garlic salt**

**Juice of 1 lime or 1 lemon**

Toss all ingredients gently in a large ceramic bowl. Transfer to serving bowl. Cover with plastic wrap and refrigerate until ready to serve.

**NOTITA:** *Create a bowl by hollowing out a vegetable (an acorn squash, for example) just for show. (You can cook the squash later, if you wish.) For individual presentation, fill large tomato shells—the color contrast is great and all is edible.*

# Ceviche

## Seafood Salad

**Makes 6 to 8 servings**

We like to blanch the fish or seafood we use in our ceviche. The real cooking, however, is accomplished by the chemical reaction of the acidic marinade upon the fish or seafood, an ancient method of fish preparation in many cultures.

**1 qt. water, boiling**

**2 lb. firm seafood (monkfish, cod, red snapper, scallops or a combination)**

**MARINADE:**

**12 Anaheim chiles, roasted, page 10, chopped**

**$1/2$ cup chopped green onion**

**$1/4$ cup garlic purée, page 12**

**1 cup chopped celery**

**2 tablespoons Tabasco sauce**

**1 tablespoon salt, or to taste**

**1 tablespoon ground black pepper, or to taste**

**1 cup chopped cilantro**

**4 tablespoons canned capers**

**1 cup fresh lime juice**

**$1/4$ cup white vinegar**

**$1/2$ cup oil**

**$1/4$ cup chopped red onion**

**1 avocado, pitted, peeled, chopped**

**GARNISH:**
Prepare the following just before serving.

**2 ripe avocados, seeded, peeled and chopped**

**8 thin slices lime**

**8 celery ribs, cut into sticks**

Several hours before serving, combine marinade ingredients in a nonreactive bowl. Next, cut seafood into $1/2$-inch cubes and blanch in boiling water a few seconds. Drain, then carefully layer the fish or seafood in a ceramic bowl alternately with the marinade. Cover with plastic wrap and refrigerate immediately. Let marinate until fish loses its translucency (at least 4 hours), stirring gently after 2 hours and again before serving.

To serve: Spoon into cocktail glasses and garnish with chopped avocado, lime slices and celery sticks.

**NOTITA:** *Modern low-calorie ceviche is made without oil and sometimes even without avocado. We love to serve ceviche on oven-baked or microwaved corn-tortilla shells with an icy-crisp lettuce mixture as a base for the delicate fish.*

# Ensalada de Elote

*Corn Salad*

**Makes 6 to 8 servings**

1 qt. water

2 (16-oz.) packages frozen yellow corn

1 teaspoon salt, or to taste

³/₄ cup Basic Vinaigrette, page 104

1 (8 oz.) can pimiento, drained and minced

1 (4 oz.) jar jalapeños, drained and minced

1 cup chopped fresh cilantro

1 teaspoon salt, or to taste

2 fresh tomatoes, minced

1 red onion, minced

Cook the corn according to package instructions; set aside to cool. In a ceramic bowl, toss the corn with Basic Vinaigrette and the remaining ingredients. Cover with plastic wrap and refrigerate 2 hours. Serve chilled as a vegetable dish or relish.

**NOTITA:** *You can also use an equivalent amount of canned kernel corn. You can improvise with garbanzo or kidney beans, or even a little Escabeche (page 62).*

# Salsa de Aguacate

*Avocado Salad Dressing*

**Makes about 4 cups**

*This is a luxurious dressing for greens, cold fish or chicken. A tablespoon or two of roasted red or green peppers, mild or hot, can also be added as a garnish.*

4 avocados, peeled, pitted

2 tablespoons lemon juice

2 cups sour cream

1 cup milk

¹/₂ teaspoon dried mustard

1 tablespoon crushed dried oregano

Dash of Tabasco sauce

1 tablespoon garlic purée, page 12

Mash avocado with lemon juice. Combine with remaining ingredients. Cover and chill. Keeps about 3 days in the refrigerator.

# Ensalada Fría de Papas

*Potato Salad*

**Makes 15 to 20 servings**

*The different combination of potatoes gives this potato salad its unusual character. You could use any one kind of potato in your version if you prefer.*

6 red potatoes

6 white potatoes

3 baking potatoes

**MARINADE DRESSING:**

1 cup vinegar

1 (10 oz.) can jalapeño strips

¹/₄ cup garlic purée, page 12

2 carrots, sliced

1 (3 oz.) jar capers, drained

1 onion sliced into rings

1 (16 oz.) jar marinated artichoke hearts; reserve marinade

1 (16 oz.) jar sliced green olives, drained

1 (16 oz.) can sliced black olives, drained

Salt and pepper to taste

**GARNISH:**

2 or 3 hard-cooked eggs, chopped

Sprigs of parsley or cilantro

Wash potatoes and cut into large chunks. Simmer in water to cover until tender but not falling apart. Cool, peel and cut into thick slices. (Leave skins on the red potatoes, if desired.)

Place marinade dressing ingredients in large glass jar, cover tightly and shake to blend ingredients. Taste and add salt and pepper, if desired.

Pour marinade over still-warm potatoes, toss gently, cover and refrigerate at least 2 hours.

# Fruit

Southwestern citrus trees produce in the winter. Winter also is also the time we get the best avocados in Tucson.

Pomegranates, meaning *apple with seeds,* are an ancient fruit and have long been used in Mexican celebrations of the New Year as a symbol of prosperity and fertility. Today they are grown commercially in California and are available mainly at Christmas time. They are the star attraction in our *Ensalada de Noche Buena,* Christmas Eve Salad, page 108.

Pomegranate syrup is unique and makes a wonderful marinade or "rub" for meat, particularly chicken. To make the syrup, I place each pomegranate on a countertop and, using my hand, roll the fruit back and forth, releasing the juice inside. I pierce one end and squeeze the juice into a nonreactive (glass) bowl, add 2 tablespoons orange juice and 2 tablespoons brown sugar to each ¹/₂ cup of pomegranate juice. (An average pomegranate yields approximately 1 cup of juice.)

# Ensalada de Espinaca

*Spinach Salad*

**Makes 12 servings**

6 navel oranges or tangerines, peeled, sectioned

1 cup seedless green grapes

4 avocados, pitted, peeled, cubed

1 red onion, sliced into thin rings

2 tablespoons vegetable, olive or walnut oil

2 bunches fresh spinach

1 cup chopped toasted pecans

1 cup crumbled Mexican cheese

Pico de Gallo seasoning, page 13

Balsamic vinegar

In a large bowl, gently toss prepared fruit, avocado cubes and onion rings with oil.

Place salad greens on individual plates or salad bowls.

Spoon fruit mixture onto greens. Top each with pecans and cheese. Pass the Balsamic vinegar and a shaker of Pico de Gallo seasoning.

**NOTITA:** *To toast pecans or other nuts, place them in a large, hot, dry skillet and, constantly stirring or shaking the pan, cook until browned lightly, or spread nuts on cookie sheet and bake at 350° F (175° C) for 10 to 15 minutes. Toasting brings out the flavor and makes the nuts crispy. Spread on toweling to cool. May be toasted in advance and stored in airtight container in the refrigerator.*

**NOTITA:** *Keep all nuts cold, even frozen, to keep them from spoiling.*

# Ensalada de Noche Buena

*Christmas Eve Salad*

**Makes 8 to 12 servings**

*Our traditional Ensalada de Noche Buena for Christmas Eve is a wonderfully colorful holiday dish that showcases winter fruit, especially the unique pomegranate, called granada. On a party table, the salad looks festive when mounded into hollow orange halves arranged on a big platter. Sometimes we sprinkle the salad with coconut.*

18 green apples

18 red apples

12 navel oranges

12 pomegranates

$^1/_2$ cup lemon juice

1 red onion, thinly sliced

1 green bell pepper, diced

$^3/_4$ cup Basic Vinaigrette, page 104

GARNISH:

1 cup walnut pieces

1 cup cubed jack cheese or Mexican cheese

1 cup seedless grapes

Shredded coconut (optional)

**NOTITA:** *The dressing for this salad can be made with infusions of vinegar with garlic or basil or by adding a squeeze of lemon juice and just a dash of oil instead of the Basic Vinaigrette.*

**LOW-FAT NOTITA:** *If you want to lower the fat and calories in the recipe, eliminate or reduce the amount of cheese, vinaigrette, walnuts and coconut.*

Wash, core and cube apples. Peel and cube oranges. (If you wish, cut oranges in half on the equator, run sharp knife around flesh to remove it and save the empty halves to be used as serving shells for the salad.) Peel and separate pomegranate sections. In a ceramic bowl combine prepared fruit with lemon juice, onion and bell pepper. Toss with Basic Vinaigrette. Cover with plastic wrap and set aside for 1 hour.

To serve: Garnish with grapes, cheese cubes, walnuts, additional dressing and a sprinkling of coconut, if desired.

**NOTITA:** *Infusions are made by steeping garlic, basil, other herbs or spices in hot vinegar. Tea is an infusion made with hot water.*

# Plato de Fruta
## *Fruit Platter*

**Makes 4 to 8 servings**

*With a sweet roll or pastry and dark, rich coffee, fruit is a lovely way to start the day. To end heavy meals, I like to serve a platter of seasonal fruits with a sprinkling of Pico de Gallo (page 13). In Mexico, especially in cities like Mazatlán and Mexico City, restaurants offer fruit platters with almost every meal. These salads include cantaloupe, honeydew and watermelon wedges, pineapple, banana and mango.*

**2 mangos**

**1 pineapple**

**¹/₂ medium Juan Canary, cantaloupe, or honeydew melon**

**4 nectarines**

**4 tablespoons grated or flaked coconut**

**2 tablespoons chopped pecans**

**Pico de Gallo seasoning, page 13**

**16 to 24 Bing cherries**

**2 limes**

Slice through pineapple lengthwise, including the leaves, if possible. (Otherwise, cut them off and, if they are good-looking, use to garnish the plate.) Cut lengthwise once again, so you have four pieces; and again for eight pieces. Cut out core section from each piece and discard. Carefully slide sharp knife under flesh, about ¹/₂ inch from pineapple shell, and remove in one piece if possible, leaving the shell intact to be used as a "boat" bowl.

Cut pineapple into bite-size pieces.

Prepare remaining fruit as desired: Peel melon and cut into chunks or balls; slice nectarines, peeled or unpeeled.

Arrange fruit in and around pineapple boats, sprinkle with coconut, nuts and a dash of Pico de Gallo seasoning mix. Garnish with cherries and lime wedges.

# Desserts
## Dulces y Postres

*At the end of your glorious Mexican meal, leave room for dessert! Dessert is sometimes overlooked, but it can be a light, refreshing way to cleanse your palate and ease your stomach. Even the diet-conscious cannot resist the thinnest sliver of fruit with just a dollop of fresh cream.*

*Prepare your postre with as much love and attention as the rest of the meal and the fond memory will linger in your guests' hearts as well as their palates.*

**Photo on pages 112-113: left to right—Flan, Capirotada, Almendrado**

# Almendrado

## Almond Meringue Pudding

**Makes 12 servings**

Almendrado is a light confection, actually an unbaked, soft meringue, molded in layers colored to resemble the Mexican flag—green, white and red (which actually is pink, in egg white). It is served with a custard sauce. It is said that if the Almendrado fails, the blame lies with the cook being angry that day.

Almendrado can be made nicely with egg substitute for the custard sauce. However, you will still need to use real egg whites for the meringue portion.

**Vegetable oil spray**

**6 egg whites at room temperature**

**1 envelope (1 scant tablespoon) unflavored gelatin**

**$^1/_4$ cup cold water**

**$^3/_4$ cup sugar**

**1 teaspoon almond extract**

**Red and green food coloring**

**$^1/_2$ cup slivered almonds**

**CUSTARD SAUCE:**

**6 egg yolks**

**$^1/_3$ cup sugar**

**Pinch salt**

**1 cup milk**

**1 cup milk or cream, additional**

**$^1/_2$ teaspoon vanilla**

**GARNISH:**

**2 cups whipped cream (sweetened if desired)**

**$^1/_2$ cup slivered almonds**

Lightly grease a loaf pan, or spray with vegetable oil and chill. Also chill a large bowl to be used to beat egg whites.

In a small saucepan, sprinkle gelatin over $^1/_4$ cup cold water. Let stand 5 minutes to soften; then place over very low heat and stir until dissolved. Set aside to cool.

Separate eggs, making sure none of the yolk contaminates the white.

In large, chilled bowl, and with oil-free, dry beaters, beat whites until firm peaks form, gradually beating in $^3/_4$ cup sugar. Beat in almond extract and cooled gelatin in a thin stream.

Place $^1/_3$ of the beaten whites into a bowl and blend in a few drops red food coloring. Spread into loaf pan. Spread half the remaining untinted whites over the pink layer. Add a few drops green food coloring to remaining whites and spread over white layer. Top with slivered almonds. Chill 2 hours, or until firm. Cover with plastic wrap after chilling so a gummy skin does not form.

Custard sauce: This sauce can be tricky. If it starts to get too thick while cooking, immediately pour it into a cool saucepan and plunge it into a pan of cold water. If the sauce is somewhat lumpy after cooking, strain it, and add milk to thin.

In a 2-quart saucepan, beat egg yolks. Add sugar, salt, milk and cream. Stir constantly over medium heat until custard thickens, about 20 minutes. Do not boil. Remove from heat; let cool. Add vanilla extract to cooled custard, or it may curdle. Pour into 1-quart pitcher, cover and chill.

Unmold Almendrado, if desired, and serve in $^3/_4$-inch-wide slices. Place a slice on a plate and drizzle custard sauce in a 2-inch-wide strip across the slice, not hiding the flag.

**Low-fat variation:** Use egg substitute and nonfat milk. Omit the whipped cream.

**NOTITA:** For special occasions, we sometimes add whipped cream and slivered almonds for garnish.

**NOTITA:** It is best to bring eggs to room temperature before using them so they will separate well. Set aside enough time to complete the dessert. If you start and are interrupted, the egg whites will fall.

# Capirotada
## *Lenten Bread Pudding*

**Makes 8 to 12 servings**

*Everyone is surprised to learn that cheese is an ingredient in this sweet, spicy concoction. Not only cheese, but onions and cilantro. You don't really taste those ingredients, but once you know they should be there, you'll miss them in any other version of bread pudding. It certainly makes a delicious dessert or breakfast.*

*Its nickname is A-Little-Bit-of-Everything-Good Pudding.*

**2 cones piloncillo, crushed, or 4 cups dark-brown sugar**

**1 qt. water**

**$^1/_2$ lb. margarine, melted**

**2 loaves French bread, sliced**

**3 cups crumbled Mexican (or jack) cheese, shredded**

**1 cup dark raisins**

**2 tablespoons chopped walnuts or pecans**

**BOUQUET GARNI WRAPPED IN CHEESECLOTH CONTAINING:**

**6 cloves**

**$^1/_4$ cup fresh cilantro**

**$^1/_4$ cup chopped green onion tops**

**3 sticks cinnamon**

**GARNISH:**

**1 pint heavy cream, whipped (sweetened, if desired)**

♦ ♦ ♦ ♦ ♦ ♦ ♦ ♦ ♦ ♦ ♦

Capirotada is considered the dish that has all the ingredients needed to fortify oneself after breaking the fast.

♦ ♦ ♦ ♦ ♦ ♦ ♦ ♦ ♦ ♦ ♦

Preheat oven to 325°F (165°C).

Boil *piloncillo* and bouquet garni in 1 quart water 10 minutes, or until syrupy.

Meanwhile, spread margarine on bread slices and toast both sides lightly under the broiler. Place half the toast in a 13 x 11-inch glass baking pan. Spread half the raisins and half the syrup over toast. Sprinkle with half the cheese. Repeat layering with remaining ingredients. Cover with foil and bake 30 minutes. Serve warm topped with whipped cream.

**NOTITA:** *Chopped apples and additional chopped nuts may be added for extra flavor and nutrition.*

# Flan
## *Caramel Custard*

**Makes 8 to 12 servings**

*Rich, smooth and delicious. I like to add a garnish, but you can serve it unadorned as well.*

**$^1/_2$ cup sugar (for caramel)**

**1 qt. scalded milk**

**6 eggs, lightly beaten**

**$^1/_4$ cup sugar**

**Pinch salt**

**1 teaspoon vanilla extract**

**GARNISH:**

**Whipped cream**

**Dash of Kahlua® liqueur**

**Slivered almonds**

Caramelize $^1/_2$ cup sugar by heating it in a skillet over very low heat, stirring constantly while it melts and turns brown. (Don't cook past this point or it will harden into amber glass!) Pour caramel into individual custard cups or pour into a 6-cup, shallow baking dish. Set aside.

Combine beaten eggs, sugar, salt and vanilla, beating well with whisk. Stir in scalded milk. Strain into baking dish over caramel coating. Place baking dish in a roasting pan and add enough hot water in the roasting pan to come halfway up the sides of the baking dish. Bake at 350°F (175°C) 20 to 30 minutes. Insert knife into center of custard. If it comes out clean, the custard is set. Cool and chill before serving, garnished with whipped cream flavored with Kahlua and almonds.

**Variation:** You can substitute other extracts in place of the vanilla.

**NOTITA:** *You'll need to make a bain marie or water bath for this custard. The shallow 6-cup baking dish you choose should fit inside a roasting pan so the custard-baking dish is surrounded with hot water while baking. If using individual custard cups, place them in one large bain marie.*

# Arroz con Leche

## Rice Pudding

**Makes 4 servings**

*A simple rice pudding is open to your own personal inter-pretation. There are no rules for rice pudding.*

**1 cup rice**

**¹/₂ stick cinnamon**

**¹/₈ teaspoon salt**

**1 cup water**

**1 cup sugar**

**³/₄ cup milk, nonfat milk or cream**

**¹/₄ cup seedless white or dark raisins**

**2 egg yolks or equivalent egg substitute**

**Grated peel from ¹/₂ lemon or orange**

**¹/₄ cup chopped almonds, pecans or pine nuts**

Combine rice, cinnamon stick and salt in 1 cup water in saucepan. Cover and bring to the boil. Reduce heat immedi-ately and steam until rice absorbs the water, about 10 minutes. Discard cinnamon stick.

Add sugar, milk and raisins to the rice, stirring lightly, not breaking up rice. Cover and let stand so milk is absorbed by rice, about 10 minutes.

Beat egg yolks and, stirring constantly, slowly stir into rice mixture.

Return to low heat and stir in peel. Cook 5 minutes more, being careful not to let the mixture burn.

Chill. Serve topped with nuts.

**NOTITA:** *A nonstick saucepan is safest.*

# Rosca de Reyes

## Three Kings Bread

**Makes one 9x5-inch loaf**

*Three Kings Bread is served on January 6, "Little Christ-mas" or* El Día de los Tres Reyes. *It is also the tradi-tional dessert for New Year's celebrations, along with* Buñuelos *(page 118). We adapted the rosca (may be translated as "ring," or maybe "twisted" or "braided") to a restaurant setting by turning it into a more cake-like pastry with butter in the batter.*

**1 lb. butter or margarine**

**1 lb. powdered sugar**

**6 eggs**

**4 cups cake flour**

**¹/₄ teaspoon baking powder**

**1 teaspoon vanilla**

**1 cup chopped walnuts or pecans**

**SYRUP:**

**2 cups brown sugar**

**1 teaspoon ground anise**

**1 teaspoon vanilla extract**

Preheat oven to 350°F (175°C).

In large mixing bowl, cream together butter or margarine and powdered sugar. Add eggs and beat again, until light and fluffy.

Combine dry ingredients, except chopped nuts.

Gradually add dry ingredi-ents and vanilla to creamed mixture.

Sprinkle nuts on bottom of lightly greased 9x5x4-inch loaf pan. Pour batter into pan on top of nuts. Bake at 350°F (175°C) 55 minutes, or until tester pick comes out clean and cake springs back to the touch. Cool 10 minutes, then turn cake out onto wire rack to cool completely.

Syrup: Melt brown sugar in heavy saucepan over low heat. Add ground anise and vanilla extract. Pour warm syrup over freshly baked cake.

★ ★ ★ ★ ★ ★ ★ ★ ★ ★ ★

Traditionally, *Rosca de Reyes* is baked with a small charm inside, such as a plastic baby figure. The one who is served the slice of bread containing the charm is obligated to give a party on Candlemass Day in February.

If you do add a charm, be sure to warn your guests to look for it!

★ ★ ★ ★ ★ ★ ★ ★ ★ ★ ★

# Mexican Bakeries

*Panaderías* or Mexican bakeries in Tucson usually are family-run. The bakeries not only bake *pan* (bread) and *pan dulce* (pastries), but stock spices, Mexican candies, coffee and cheese, as well as Mexican periodicals, just as a typical corner store would.

*Pan dulce* is made of yeast dough that is shaped in many styles and flavored with varying spices. They resemble Danish pastries and are served with coffee for breakfast.

*Left to right—Pumpkin Tamal with Pineapple Chutney, Empanadas de Manzana, Chocolate Caliente*

# Tamales de Calabaza
## Sweet Pumpkin Tamales

Makes 24 tamales

*For breakfast on the Dia de los Muertos, serve these special tamales. Ideally these are eaten alone, for breakfast or a late-afternoon snack, along with coffee or hot chocolate. If fresh masa is available, use it and omit the chicken broth.*

MASA:

$3/4$ cup vegetable shortening

1 cup sugar

1 teaspoon salt

2 teaspoons baking powder

$3 1/2$ cups (1 lb.) premixed masa

$2 1/2$ cups warm chicken broth

FILLING:

$1 1/2$ cups (16 oz.) canned pumpkin

1 (5 oz.) can evaporated milk

$3/4$ cup sugar

2 teaspoons ground cinnamon

$1/2$ teaspoon ground nutmeg

1 teaspoon vanilla extract

$1/2$ cup coconut

$1/2$ cup crushed pineapple

$1/4$ cup chopped pecans or raisins, optional

Dried corn husks

Pineapple Chutney, recipe follows

For masa: Whip vegetable shortening until fluffy, about 5 minutes. Beat in sugar, salt and baking powder. Add premixed masa and broth alternately, beating until well mixed. Let stand at room temperature 5 minutes.

For filling: In a saucepan, combine pumpkin, milk, sugar, cinnamon and nutmeg. Over medium heat, bring to a boil and cook for one minute. Remove from heat. Stir in vanilla extract, coconut, pineapple and pecans or raisins, if using. Set mixture aside to cool completely.

To assemble: Soak corn husks in hot water about 30 minutes, to soften. Remove and wipe off extra water. Separate corn husks. In center of each husk, spread about 2 tablespoons masa. Spoon 1 tablespoon filling lengthwise down center of masa. Fold husk over filling to encase it. (Use two husks if necessary.) Fold bottom, pointed end up, over enclosed filling. (See illustration on page 33.) Place tamales, open end up, in a steamer basket or Dutch oven fitted with a rack. Do not crowd. If necessary, place extra husks among tamales to keep them upright. Place a layer of husks over tamales; cover and steam about 1-$1/4$ to 1-$1/2$ hours. To serve, open husks and top with 2 tablespoons of warm pineapple chutney.

# Cajeta de Piña
## Pineapple Chutney

Makes enough chutney to garnish 24 pumpkin tamales

1 (16-oz.) jar pineapple preserves or jam

1 teaspoon fresh orange zest

3 tablespoons whole-cranberry sauce, optional

1 cup shredded coconut

Place pineapple preserves, fresh orange zest and cranberry sauce, if using, in a microwave dish and heat. Stir to blend. Add coconut.

Use immediently or keep in refrigerator for up to one week. Reheat before using.

# Buñuelos
## New-Year Pastry

Makes 24 buñuelos

*Eggs, milk, butter and sugar produce an incredibly rich delicacy called buñuelos. These must be eaten as soon as fried, although the dough itself can be made a few hours ahead. Honey may be substituted for the syrup.*

2 cups flour

$1/2$ teaspoon baking powder

$1/2$ teaspoon salt

2 eggs, beaten

$1/4$ cup butter, softened

$3/4$ cup milk or water

2 cups oil, for frying

SYRUP:

2 cones piloncillo, crushed, or 4 cups dark-brown sugar

1 stick cinnamon

2 cups water

GARNISH:

2 cups heavy cream, whipped (sweetened, if desired)

$1/2$ cup chopped walnuts

Sift together dry ingredients. Add beaten eggs, butter, milk and as much of the flour as will be absorbed. Knead. Divide into 24 balls the size of limes. Press or roll with a rolling pin to 4 or 5 inches in diameter. Heat oil to deep-frying temperature and fry each buñuelo on both sides until a delicate brown. Drain on paper towels. Serve with syrup and garnish.

Syrup: Crumble *piloncillo,* combine with cinnamon and

water, and boil until thickened. Pour over hot buñuelos, garnish with whipped cream and nuts and serve at once.

# Galletas
## Mexican Wedding Cookies

**Makes 24 cookies**

*Some cultures add pepper or anise to this timeless recipe. They are so delicate they seem to pop and disappear in the mouth. In Mexico and in Tucson, guests at weddings are invited to take home a few cookies after the fiesta. They are token thank-you gifts from the families of the nuptial couple.*

**2 cups all-purpose flour**

**1$^1$/$_4$ cups powdered sugar, divided**

**1 cup soft margarine or butter**

**1 teaspoon vanilla extract**

**$^1$/$_4$ teaspoon salt**

**1 cup finely chopped or coarsely ground almonds**

Preheat oven to 325°F (165°C).

In a large bowl, beat together margarine or butter, $^1$/$_2$ cup of the powdered sugar and vanilla until light and fluffy.

Combine flour, salt and chopped almonds. Gradually, but quickly, add flour mixture to creamed mixture and mix on low speed just until partially blended. Turn dough onto board and knead by hand with a light touch until well blended. The less handling, the better. Form 1-inch balls. Place balls on ungreased cookie sheets and bake 15 to 20 minutes until set, but not brown. Cool slightly, then roll each ball in remaining powdered sugar. Cool completely and roll them a second time in the powdered sugar. Store in airtight containers or freeze.

**NOTITA:** *The dough can be rolled $^1$/$_4$-inch thick and cut into small crescents, circles or other shapes.*

**Chocolate variation:** To make a chocolate version of Mexican Wedding Cookies, add an extra tablespoon butter or margarine along with unsweetened cocoa. Combine the same amount of cocoa as powdered sugar (1$^1$/$_4$ cups each, divided) in the batter as well as to the coating in which the baked cookies are rolled.

# Galletitas de Almendra
## Almond Cookies

**Makes about 36 cookies**

*This is an old, old recipe I found in my grandmother's hand-written recipe book. We loved these oat-and-almond cookies when we were children.*

**1$^3$/$_4$ cups all-purpose flour**

**$^1$/$_4$ teaspoon salt**

**1 cup softened butter or margarine**

**1 cup powdered sugar**

**1 teaspoon almond extract**

**$^3$/$_4$ cup ground almonds**

**1 cup uncooked oats**

**Additional powdered sugar**

Preheat oven to 325°F (165°C).

Combine flour and salt and set aside.

In a large bowl, beat butter or margarine with powdered sugar until light and fluffy. Beat in almond extract.

Gradually stir in flour and salt mixture, mixing well. Then stir in ground almonds and oatmeal just until incorporated.

Shape dough into crescents using walnut-size balls of dough. Bake 10 to 15 minutes on ungreased cookie sheet. Remove to rack and cool. Roll cookies in the additional powdered sugar. Store tightly covered, or freeze.

On November 1 and 2, many Mexican people pay homage to the departed. They spend time at the gravesites with the deceased, sharing food, decorating graves, offering toasts and burning incense. On the Día de los Muertos (Day of the Dead), the departed return from beyond to visit their relatives on earth. The living greet them happily with music and everything the dead person enjoyed in life. It is a time of joy.

To prepare for the occasion, bakers work for days to make special breads, flower growers provide their bright flowers, and confectioners produce a variety of sweets shaped into coffins, rabbits, lambs and other figures. At El Charro, we serve pumpkin tamales as well as **Los Muertos** bread.

# Bizcochuelos

## *Anise Cookies*

**Makes about 12 cookies**

*Although we associate these tasty morsels with Christmas, they are wonderful any time of the year.*

$^1/_2$ *cup butter*

$^1/_2$ *sugar*

*1 egg*

$^1/_2$ *teaspoon ground anise*

*1 tablespoon brandy*

$1^1/_2$ *cups cake flour*

*1 teaspoon baking powder*

$^1/_4$ *teaspoon salt*

$^1/_4$ *cup light-brown sugar*

$^1/_2$ *teaspoon ground cinnamon*

Preheat oven to 350°F (175°C).

Cream together butter and sugar. Add egg and continue beating until fluffy. Add brandy.

Combine dry ingredients (except brown sugar and cinnamon). Gradually add dry ingredients to creamed mixture, mixing until well blended.

Turn out dough onto waxed paper and knead lightly. Form dough into a ball. Refrigerate dough, wrapped in plastic, for at least one hour.

Roll out dough to $^1/_4$ inch thick. With wreath-shaped cookie cutter or doughnut cutter, cut as many cookies as possible and place on ungreased cookie sheet. Reroll remaining dough and repeat cutting process. Sprinkle cookies with brown sugar and cinnamon mixture.

Bake at 350°F (175°C) for about 12 minutes, or until cookies are firm and starting to brown.

Remove cookies to wire rack and cool before storing.

**NOTITA:** *Dough may be made up to 3 days ahead of baking.*

# Empanadas de Manzana

## *Apple Turnovers*

**Makes 8 servings**

*For a chunkier filling, cook the sauce until the apples are just tender. They will continue to soften while baking.*

***Empanada Pastry, page 82***

**APPLE FILLING:**

*3 tart apples, peeled, cored and chopped*

$^1/_2$ *cup sugar (to start)*

*Scant $^1/_8$ teaspoon salt*

*Juice of 1 lemon*

$^1/_2$ *teaspoon cinnamon*

$^1/_4$ *teaspoon ground cloves*

**EGG WASH (optional):**

*1 egg*

*2 tablespoons water*

Prepare Empanada Pastry.

Preheat oven to 400°F (200°C).

Combine Apple Filling ingredients in a saucepan. Cook over medium heat, stirring occasionally, until apples are barely tender. Set aside.

Cut rounds of pastry about 4 inches in diameter. Place 1 or 2 tablespoons of filling on lower half of circle. Fold bottom half up and over the filling, and press together upper edges of the half-circle with the tines of a fork to seal. Prepare egg wash, if desired, by beating together egg and water.

Brush empanadas with egg wash, if desired, and sprinkle with sugar. Place filled empanadas on an ungreased baking sheet and bake at 400°F (200°C) 15 to 20 minutes or until pastry is nicely browned. Remove to wire rack to cool or serve warm.

## Empanadas Dulces de Fruta — Fruit-filled Turnovers

The **empanada** is a classic Mexican dish, another that probably bears French influence. It can be rough and peasant-like or gussied up with fancy fillings and a decorative edging. You'll find **empanadas** in every **panadería,** filled with the pumpkin and apple preparations that are favored. But anything from canned pumpkin-pie mix to jarred applesauce and fruit preserves to homemade fruit fillings are found inside **empanadas dulces.** They make wonderful take-along sweets for lunch boxes or picnics.

Left to right—Bizcochuelos, Galletitas de Almendra, Galletas

# Cocadas
## Macaroons

Makes 12 cookies

Monica often served a light dessert after a heavy meal. Meringues and macaroons with coffee for adults, and hot chocolate for the children, were served up in great style by our Tía.

**3 cups blanched almonds, coarsely chopped**
**³/₄ cups sugar**
**10 egg whites**

Preheat oven to 350°F (175°C).

Grind almonds and sugar together. Gradually add egg whites to make a soft dough. Drop by teaspoonfuls on cookie sheet lined with waxed paper or parchment. Bake at 350°F (175°C) 8 to 10 minutes or until set and showing tips of light brown.

# Los Besos del Angel
## Meringues

Makes 6 meringues

Closely related to macaroons are meringues. I believe they are in Tucson's repertoire because of the many Jewish settlers of French and German cultural ancestry who have enriched the city for more than 100 years.

Anyone who ever has struggled with flopped egg whites will love to make them in Tucson, where we have 10 and 12 percent humidity most of the year.

Meringues don't really bake; they dry out. That's why they are cooked in what used to be called a "slow" oven.

**6 egg whites at room temperature**
**¹/₂ teaspoon cream of tartar**
**1 teaspoon almond extract**
**1¹/₂ cups sugar**

Preheat oven to 225°F (110°C).

Line a baking sheet with brown paper or parchment that has been coated with butter and floured.

Beat egg whites and cream of tartar until soft peaks form. Add almond extract. Stir in sugar gradually. Place meringue mixture in pastry bag and pipe rounds onto prepared baking sheet. Quickly place in oven for about 45 minutes or until meringues are dry. Cool completely and store in an air-tight container for up to a week.

# Drinks

## Bebidas

*The Flin home, now El Charro Café, was built by my great-grandfather, Jules Flin, in about 1896. The high-ceilinged house is made of the black volcanic basalt rock that characterize most of Flin's buildings around Tucson.*

*The Court Street house was lively, with children and adults coming and going. On Sundays it was the custom for single young men and women to mingle at afternoon socials in various homes. The Flin home was a popular gathering place. I imagine the wide wooden porch would groan under the dancing done by the young people, who would be sipping* horchata *or* tamarindo *or lemonade and singing along to a young man's mandolin or guitar.*

*Some of those same refrescos from Monica's childhood were given to us when we had summer colds. We still swear by them. Tía Mamie would bring them to us in gallon-size glass jars. The refrescos soothed our fevers and cooled us off.*

Photos on page 124-125; left to right -Panche, El Charro Margarita de Casa, Jamaca

# Horchata (Agua de Arroz)
## Rice-Water Cooler

**Makes 12 servings**

*For hundreds of years, mothers have known that rice can help babies with bad tummies once in a while. Here is a drink that soothes babes in arms and is a picker-upper for Mamá and Papi as well. Most babies would prefer the rice drink without so much sugar and no cinnamon.*

**1$^1$/$_2$ qt. water**

**4 cups rice**

**Cinnamon sticks (enough for each person)**

**1 qt. nonfat milk**

**2 cups sugar**

**2 qt. additional water**

**Ground cinnamon or nutmeg**

Soak rice in 1$^1$/$_2$ quarts water for 4 hours. Drain.

A batch at a time, purée the rice in a blender with some of the milk.

The rice will not be completely puréed, so strain the mixture well, discarding the hard bits of rice, and reserving the milky extract.

Next, dissolve sugar in additional 2 quarts water. Combine with rice and milk mixture. Refrigerate before serving. Serve over ice and top with ground cinnamon or nutmeg, if desired.

**NOTITA:** *Use a cinnamon stick in each glass as a stirrer.*

# Horchata de Coco
## Coconut Drink

**Makes about 3 quarts**

*The first time I made horchata it was for my children, because I didn't want to serve them soft drinks.*

**1 large coconut**

**2 qt. scalding water**

**2 cups sugar**

**Chopped ice**

Grind and sift the coconut meat. Place in a heatproof container with scalding water. Set aside. When cold, strain. Add sugar and chopped ice.

**Variation:** Substitute 3 cups of watermelon pulp for the coconut to make a watermelon drink.

**NOTITA:** *Adjust the amount of sugar to suit your own taste.*

# Tamarindo
## Tamarind Drink

**Makes about 6 quarts**

*Surprise your guests and serve this refreshing drink after they've had a Mexican dinner.*

**$^1$/$_2$ lb. tamarinds, peeled and cut in half**

**2 cups water**

**2 cups sugar**

**5$^1$/$_2$ qt. water**

**Ice**

**Mint sprigs, slices of lemon or orange**

In saucepan, place tamarinds with 2 cups cold water. Bring to the boil. Reduce heat and simmer gently for 15 minutes. Set aside. When cool, remove tamarinds. Strain liquid into large pitcher. Stir in sugar. Add remaining water.

Serve with ice and a sprig of mint or slices of lemon or orange.

# Jamaica
## *Hibiscus Drink*

**Makes about 6 quarts**

Red hibiscus petals are the source of the beautiful color as well as the flavor. Jamaica is also served hot, like tea.

**¹/₂ lb. jamaica petals (found in produce department)**

**6 qt. of water**

**2 cups sugar**

**Ice**

**Orange slices**

Wash the jamaica petals. Boil 1 quart of water and add the jamaica petals. Set aside for 2 hours. Strain, then add sugar and the rest of the water. Serve with ice and orange slices.

## Tucson's Mariachi Festival

One of the largest celebrations in town is held in conjunction with Tucson's world-famous Mariachi Festival each April. For half a week, youngsters in Tucson attend workshops put on by professional mariachi musicians from Mexico and the United States. One night is designated Garibaldi Night (after Plaza Garibaldi, the famous fiesta site in Mexico City) and the city sets up rows of food booths in Armory Park downtown. Visiting mariachi groups play on two stages. Everyone goes to listen to the energizing music and eat all kinds of food, from Mexican to Japanese. The Mariachi Festival culminates in a stupendous concert in the Tucson Convention Center Arena headlined by a big star, often Tucson's own Linda Ronstadt.

# Hot Chocolate

Mexicans have never done much with their native chocolate except drink it. Moctezuma fed Hernán Cortés *atoles*, a hot, thick beverage made with corn meal and chocolate sweetened with honey—which he probably didn't like any more than I do.

The chocolate we use for hot chocolate is made by the Ibarra company. It contains chocolate, cinnamon and raw sugar, which makes it gritty and unique among chocolates.

# Chocolate Caliente
## *Beaten Hot Chocolate*

**Makes 3 to 6 servings**

*I wish I didn't have to put in a warning about salmonella poisoning from raw eggs. You might feel more comfortable using pasteurized egg substitute in place of the egg yolk and forgetting about the lovely froth contributed by the fluffed egg whites.*

**4 tablespoons cocoa (or 4 squares Ibarra Mexican chocolate)**

**3 cups whole milk (or 12 oz. evaporated milk and 12 oz. water)**

**1 cup sugar**

**Pinch of salt**

**3 eggs, separated**

**1 teaspoon vanilla extract**

**Ground cinnamon, optional**

Dissolve cocoa in small amount of water (or melt chocolate squares over hot water). Place in saucepan and stir in milk (or evaporated milk and water), sugar and salt. Cook over medium heat until mixture comes to the boil. Set aside.

Beat egg yolks until thick and lemon-colored. Beat whites until stiff and fold into yolks. Add vanilla. Add egg mixture to chocolate mixture. Whip with a *molinillo* (the traditional whisk made of decoratively carved wood) or a wire whisk and serve with a sprinkle of ground cinnamon.

# Tequila to ¡Toma!

### Salud, dinero y amor,
### y tiempo para gozarlos

### —Health, money and love,
### and the time to enjoy them

*¡Toma!* means *to drink* in Spanish. It is a single word that is translated into myriad expressions. *¡Toma!* is to drink with gusto, enjoyment and passion. It is this spirit I wanted to express with the opening of our ¡Toma! Cantina®. As you walk through the artfully painted "nesting" rooms of the cantina, you can feel that love of life we aimed to capture.

The beautiful bold colors, wrought-iron and wood furniture, and paintings from some of Tucson's best artists, coupled with our extensive fine-tequila collection, helps make ¡Toma! more than a cantina.

*¡Pa arriba, pa abajo, para centro, para dentro!* ("Up, down, center and down the hatch" is a rough translation of this traditional Mexican toast.) *¡Salud!*

## About Tequila

In the well at the heart *(piña)* of the giant agave or century plant is a thick yellow liquid, *miel* (honey), that is used medicinally; fermented, it becomes the potent *pulque*. Further refined, it becomes mezcal and tequila.

The agave is a member of the lily family. It is not a type of cactus, as is commonly thought.

The production of tequila in its many varieties is strictly regulated by the Mexican government and can be made from agave grown only in five areas of Mexico. The liquid extracted from the *piña* of the agave is aged in oak barrels, sometimes for a year.

# El Charro Margarita de Casa

Makes 1 large pint-glass serving

Fruit, such as fresh strawberries, peaches, mangos, and raspberries may be an added twist, served in a sugar-rimmed glass.

Margaritas are lovely served in Mexican hand-blown, blue-rimmed glasses.

*¹/₂ part Sauza® Giro*
*¹/₂ part Sauza® Silver*
*2 parts Sauza® Mix*
*Splash of Triple Sec*
*Squeeze of lime juice*
*Splash of orange juice*
*Lime wedge, optional*

Combine all ingredients and serve over ice cubes in a salt-rimmed margarita glass. Add lime wedge, if using.

NOTITA: *For purists, the traditional El Charro method is to serve Margaritas on the rocks (over ice) in a salt-rimmed glass with a wedge of lime. Margaritas may be frozen—combined with crushed ice rather than ice cubes—but they tend to become watery that way and it is hard to capture the true taste of the tequila.*

# Ponche

## Eggnog

Makes 4 to 6 servings

Whenever Monica felt like giving a Christmas party for El Charro employees in the 1940s and '50s, she would serve this rich eggnog along with homemade cookies.

*1 qt. milk*
*2 teaspoons sugar*
*¹/₂ teaspoon ground cinnamon*
*1 egg (pasteurized) or ¹/₄ cup egg substitute*
*¹/₂ cup brandy or dark rum*
GARNISH:
*1 cup whipped cream*
*Several cinnamon sticks*

Heat milk until bubbles form around edges of saucepan. Add sugar and ground cinnamon. Beat egg until frothy and add to milk. Stir in brandy or rum. Garnish with whipped cream and serve each cup with a cinnamon-stick stirrer.

# Sangría de Flores

## Flores Family Wine Punch

Makes 8 to 10 cups

Serve this linda Sangría in Hacienda-style glassware, which is stout and rimmed with blue, and float some rose petals in each glass.

Sangría, which has hundreds of variations, actually seems to have been conceived in Spain. Here's our family's favorite.

*1 bottle red burgundy wine*
*¹/₂ bottle of Presidente Brandy®*
*³/₄ cup orange juice*
*³/₄ cup grapefruit juice*
*³/₄ cup cranberry juice*
*Juice of 4 limes*
GARNISH:
*1 cup chopped apple*
*1 cup chopped orange segments*
*1 cup chopped cantaloupe*
*1 cup rose petals (optional)*

In a punch bowl, combine all the beverages. Add chopped fruit just before serving.

NOTITA: *To keep the punch cool without diluting it, freeze an extra quart of one of the juices in a ring mold. Add the frozen juice to the punch and it will float prettily.*

~WATCH YOUR HEAD~

# Spanish Glossary

*In Spanish, words ending in a vowel, N or S are accented on the next-to-the-last syllable, unless there is a written accent mark:* **que**so, fi**es**tas, a**mi**go, **ta**co; *but* te**lé**fono. *Those ending with consonants other than those Ns or Ss are stressed on the last syllable:* profe**sor**, ta**mal**. *(An exception is* resto**rán**.)*Two Ls are pronounced like "Y"; QU is prounounced "K;" Rs are trilled and Gs are pronounced "heh," with a throaty gurgle—but you will be understood graciously if you don't have these skills, and* por fa**vor** *will get you almost anything.*

**aceite.** Cooking oil.

**aceituna.** Olive.

**adobo.** Seasoning sauce or marinade made of red chiles ground to a paste, seasoned with vinegar and herbs.

**agua.** Water.

**aguacate.** Avocado or alligator pear. Those with coarse, dark skin are better-tasting than the shiny, pale-green ones, which tend to be watery and lack flavor.

**ajo.** Garlic; so important, we named a town in western Arizona after it.

**albóndigas.** Meatballs.

**al horno.** Oven-baked.

**ancho.** A poblano chile that has been dried and has turned a black-red color; means "wide."

**antojito.** An hors d'oeuvre or small snack food.

**arroz.** Rice.

**asar.** To roast or broil.

**azucar.** Sugar.

**barbacoa.** Barbecued meat.

**borracho.** Cooked with beer or wine. Means "drunk."

**buñuelo.** Puffy, sweet, deep-fried pastry.

**burro.** Large flour tortilla wrapped around a filling.

**calabaza.** Squash, pumpkin.

**caldo.** Soup, broth.

**caliente.** Hot to the touch (temperature); *picante* is spicy hot.

**camarón.** Shrimp.

**camote.** Sweet potato.

**canela.** Cinnamon.

**capirotada.** Spicy bread pudding served during Lent; means "a little bit of everything."

**carne.** Meat, specifically beef.

**carne seca.** Dried beef jerky, shredded and spiced.

**cazuela.** A stew pot; at El Charro, the name of a hearty bowl of "dry" beef soup.

**cebolla.** Onion.

**cerveza.** Beer; *cerveza fría* is cold beer.

**ceviche.** Salad made of fish "cooked" in lime juice.

**chalupa.** Corn masa tart, fried, then topped with meat, fish, beans or vegetables. Means "canoe."

**chilaquiles.** Corn tortilla pieces covered with enchilada sauce and cheese and baked in a casserole.

**chile.** We use the Spanish spelling for pepper; the Spanish interpreted the sound "chil" used by the Aztecs for hot peppers. Other writers choose *chili,* insisting "Chile"

is the name of a country.

**chili powder.** Commercially, the product made from ground red chiles and including a variety of other spices.

**chimichanga.** Deep-fried burro; means "thingamajig."

**chorizo.** Pork or beef sausage.

**chuleta.** Chop or cutlet.

**cilantro.** Coriander or Chinese parsley.

**coco.** Coconut.

**comal.** Heavy, round griddle for baking tortillas.

**con.** With; as.

**ejote.** String bean.

**elote.** Corn; sometimes *helote.*

**empanada.** Pastry turnover.

**enchilada.** A corn tortilla usually dipped in red chile sauce, rolled around just about anything, then topped with more sauce and cheese and baked; Enchiladas Sonorenses (page 27) are not rolled.

**enrollado.** Rolled.

**ensalada.** Salad.

**escabeche.** Pickle.

**fideos.** Vermicelli; thin pasta.

**flan.** Baked custard with caramel coating.

**flauta.** Corn tortilla tightly rolled around a filling, then deep-fried; means "flute."

**frijoles.** Beans, usually pinto beans.

**gallina.** Hen.

**garbanzo.** Chickpea.

**gazpacho.** Cold, spicy tomato soup.

**granada.** Pomegranate.

**guacamole.** Mashed avocado salad or dip.

**guajolote.** In Mexico, turkey.

**harina.** Wheat flour.

**hoja.** Corn husk, used to wrap tamales; sometimes *oja.*

**hongo.** Mushroom.

**huevo.** Egg; also *blanquillo.*

**jamón.** Ham.

**jícama.** When peeled, a crisp, white, edible root.

**Kahlúa.** Coffee-flavored liqueur made in Mexico.

**lechuga.** Lettuce.

**lima.** Lime.

**limón.** Lemon.

**maíz.** Corn.

**mano.** A piece of volcanic rock used with both hands to grind food against another rock; also, "hard," "hand."

**manteca.** Lard.

**mantequilla.** Butter.

**mariscos.** Shellfish. Fish is *pescado.*

**masa.** Dough, usually referring to ground hominy, called *nixtamal.*

**menudo.** Tripe soup; traditional on New Year's Day to ease hangovers.

**metate.** Slab of volcanic rock on three legs used for grinding corn. In the old days, the one in El Charro's kitchen was used to shred *carne seca.*

**miel.** Honey.

**molcajete.** Volcanic rock shaped like a bowl in which food is ground.

**mole.** Unsweetened chocolate-and-chile sauce.

**molinillo.** Hot chocolate beater, usually made of wood and beautifully carved.

**naranja.** Orange.

**nixtamal.** Hominy; raw corn grains, soaked in lime, then ground to make a dough (*masa*) for tortillas, tamales, chalupas.

**nopales.** Prickly-pear cactus pads cooked and used in fresh salads or cooked as a vegetable.

**o.** Or.

**olla.** Clay pot; especially, a pot in which beans are simmered.

**pan.** Bread.

**pastel.** Pie.

**pechuga de pollo.** Breast of chicken.

**pepino.** Cucumber.

**pescado.** Fish other than shellfish (*mariscos*).

**picadillo.** Meat hash; literally, "cut up."

**picante.** Hot to the taste buds.

**pico de gallo.** Rooster's beak, referring playfully to the hot-and-spicy mixture we sprinkle over fresh fruit (page 109). In some areas, including Tucson, *pico de gallo* refers to a tomato-and-chile salsa.

**piloncillo.** Brown sugar formed into a cone for commercial sale.

**pimiento.** Red pepper; also *pimento.*

**pinoñes.** Pine nuts; also seen as *pignoles.*

**pipián.** A sauce made of pumpkin seed, chile and spices.

**poblano.** A variety of green chile, wide for stuffing.

**pollo.** Chicken; *pechuga* refers to chicken breast.

**postre.** Dessert.

**quelites.** Spinach; sometimes, any green-leaf vegetable.

**quesadilla.** Grilled-cheese sandwich made with a tortilla.

**queso.** Cheese; *queso fresco* is unaged cheese.

**rábano.** Radish.

**rajas.** Thin strips, as in thin strips of chile.

**relleno.** Stuffed.

**repollo.** Cabbage.

**ristra.** String of dried red chiles; also, *sarta.*

**sal.** Salt; *sin sal* means without salt, useful to know when ordering a tequila-and-lime-juice cocktail called a *margarita* (daisy), which usually is served in a salt-rimmed glass.

**salsa.** Sauce.

**sangría.** A drink made of red wine, brandy, sugar, oranges, lemons and apples.

**seco.** Dry.

**sopa.** Soup.

**sopa seca.** Literally, a "dry soup," indicating a dish made with rice or a pasta that absorbs most of the cooking liquid.

**taco.** A U-shaped corn tortilla with filling.

**tamal (pl. tamales).** A corn husk filled with masa, meat or beans.

**tatemar** (verb). To roast, peel and seed green chiles.

**tejolote.** Pestle.

**tequila.** Distilled liquor made from agave (century plant).

**topopo.** A salad shaped like a volcano or pyramid.

**torta.** Pie or pastry; omelet.

**tortilla.** A thin, flat bread made from either wheat flour (*harina*) or corn masa (*nixtamal*).

**tostada.** Toasted; specifically, toasted tortillas.

**totopos.** Corn tortillas cut into triangles and fried in lard; also known as *tortilla chips.*

**totopitos.** Our name for the same totopos, but cut into matchsticks and fried for garnish on soups or salads.

# Index

Bold-type page numbers refer to recipes.

134